MONT

FOR PARENTS

A Complete Guide to Creating a Montessori Home and Raising a Montessori Child for Parents of Infants, Toddlers, Tweens, Teens, Young Adults, and Everyone in Between

Beatrice Bell

Contents

Introduction

As parents, we just want one thing— for our children to be happy, successful, and thriving. However, it is no secret that the parenting journey is filled with various challenges, so you can often find yourself asking, "*Am I doing what is best for my child? Am I doing enough regarding involvement, education, and discipline?*" And, more importantly, "*Do I have the power to change something and help my children maximize their potential in a safe, naturally paced, and supportive way?*"

Let me tell you one thing—you wield more power than you can imagine; you just need the right strategy to implement it. So, allow me to present you with the Montessori education, its philosophy, and what benefits you and your child will enjoy.

Montessori education philosophy and benefits for children of ALL ages

Before you think this model is based on strict rules and regulations that cause anxiety and irritability, you can relax and forget your experiences related to general approaches.

There is no one-size-fits-all for parenting and education—your loved ones are unique and deserve something tailored to their personality. That, my devoted parents, is the beauty of the Montessori education philosophy—it honors your child's authenticity and is self-paced. Naturally, it is still a guided approach, masterfully assessed, fully immersed in creative ways to elevate their knowledge while thriving in a supportive and nurturing surrounding.

This revolutionary way of shaping young, curious minds was created a century ago by Dr. Maria Montessori, an Italian physician. Today, her methods have completely reshaped various schools worldwide. The philosophy revolves around deeply diving into self-motivated growth through multi-sensory learning and a child-centered approach. Because it embraces a teaching that allows the children to develop at their own pace, it further stimulates their curiosity to understand and achieve their personal goals. They are encouraged to make connections, collaborate, and critically question things, becoming accountable and confident persons who are independent, self-directed learners. Isn't that what every parent wants for their children?

Let us dive more deeply into the benefits of the Montessori educational model. But remember, the following advantages are just the tip of the iceberg.

Becoming capable

A primary driving force of this educational approach is developing capabilities—regardless of age. Whether it is potty training, solving math equations, or solving problems in a group, every goal has its own creative approach through various developmental activities. But how does this method differ from other school teachings? Montessori schools have classrooms that feature one of each activity. This is important as it gives children the freedom to choose what they wish to engage in and make the most of what is available—they can choose to work in a group or solo. Moreover, the classrooms don't have only one age; they comprise different ages, which opens the possibility of building interpersonal communication and relationships.

Becoming accountable

Through Montessori learning, children take charge by choosing and progressing in their activities and doing so at their own pace. That makes them accountable for the knowledge they have gained. With so many options to practice and review their progress or simply level up and move toward mastering another activity, children eagerly achieve their individualized goals. If unsatisfied with their progress, they are also taught to self-assess, self-correct, and develop critical opinions to learn from their errors. This means they become accountable for their learning curve.

Becoming knowledgeable

The approach nurtures the aspect of self-educating with guidance, but also to really think about the gained knowledge through a creative sensory process. It is a hands-on experience encouraging deep understanding and eventually evolves toward more complex lessons. For that reason, the curriculum groups children into 3-year cycles instead of the traditional year-by-year expectations. It is focused on the milestones of different development periods—no child is the same, and one cannot expect the same outcome from every individual in such a short yearly period. In other words, the Montessori curriculum respects that children's growth unfolds differently, and its responsibility is to provide the right tools and safe space for the children to evolve when they are encouraged and ready.

Gaining a sense of self

Because Montessori schools practice grouping different age groups as per the 3-year cycles, taught by the same teacher, they not only have a role in building a community and bonds, but they also start to understand everyone has individual needs. As a result, they start to acknowledge their own, exploring themselves and their independence. Furthermore, as they advance and master the skills, they can mentor other children and learn how to care for and support those who need their help.

Generally, children become incredibly confident in choosing learning activities based on their needs, explore their authenticity, become inquisitive, and, most of all, creative. When you give children the freedom to take their own actions, you are helping them build themselves as strong and capable persons.

The challenges of not being able to attend a Montessori school

Of course, not every parent has the option to send their child to a Montessori school. Be it for financial reasons, filled positions, or any other—your loved ones might be missing out on some incredible opportunities. Some of the challenges that may arise include not being able to get hands-on learning in a traditional educational system, almost no chance of getting individualized learning options, missing the chance to develop practical life skills like cleaning or cooking, missing the opportunity to build mixed-age relationships, and no access to the Montessori learning principles which are not incorporated in other schools.

But that's why I am here. My book aims to show you how the Montessori educational principles can be adopted at home when Montessori schooling isn't necessarily available—regardless of your child's age. This reading journey will give you all the essentials you need to know, as well as how to incorporate ideas on developmental milestones and promote the Montessori principles at home. You will learn how to organize and optimize your home, what to pay attention to, how to deal with particular challenges, and experience first-hand why Montessori education is incredibly beneficial for your child.

Chapter 1:
Understanding Montessori Philosophy

I know you are already eager to learn all the approaches that can transform your parenthood for the better, but to do that, we must plunge into its origins and understand the core essence.

Throughout the evolution of modern man, there have been plenty of changes in many aspects of life—education included. In essence, the changes in the educational system tend to reflect their time, meaning that each of them has emerged as a result of a certain social context. And this is exactly what made Maria Montessori come up with her own unique approach when it comes to schooling children.

When she was growing up, the education system was pretty harsh. Classrooms looked more like factories instead of places that induced children's creativity. Force-feeding knowledge was the only approach teachers knew of, and punishment was the ultimate tool to 'encourage' them to learn more.

So, how did this woman become inspired and created a new, improved schooling method? Understanding her revolutionary perspective requires having a basic understanding of her life's events.

The Life of Maria Montessori

Childhood and education

Maria Montessori, born on August 31, 1870, in Chiaravalle, Italy, had a childhood marked by curiosity and determination. Growing up in a supportive and progressive family, she displayed a keen interest in science and mathematics from an early age. In a time when girls were often discouraged from pursuing education, her parents, especially her father, recognized her potential and encouraged her academic pursuits. This encouragement set the stage for Maria's remarkable educational journey.

Montessori's formal education was initially focused on engineering, a field typically reserved for men. However, her passion led her to defy societal norms and become one of the first female students to enroll in the University of Rome's medical school. She not only excelled in her studies but also became a trailblazer by earning her medical degree in 1896. She began studying pedagogy and child development when she was still a medical student, a decision that would shape the course of her life and contribute to the development of the Montessori method, an innovative and child-centered approach to education that continues to influence educational practices worldwide.

The birth of her unique approach

Maria Montessori initially focused her medical practice on psychiatry, but her growing interest in education led her to attend pedagogy classes, deepening her understanding of educational theory. This newfound passion inspired her to scrutinize the quality of education provided to children with disabilities, encompassing both intellectual and developmental aspects.

In 1900, she received a pivotal opportunity when she was appointed co-director of a groundbreaking institute for special education teachers. Here, she adopted an experimental approach, meticulously observing and assessing various teaching methods to determine their effectiveness. Her dedication significantly improved the children's learning outcomes, establishing the program as a resounding success.

In 1907, Maria Montessori established Italy's first full-day childcare center in the San Lorenzo district of Rome. This pioneering institution catered to children aged 3 to 7 whose parents were at work during the day. Known as the Casa dei Bambini, it combined quality learning with a nurturing environment, setting a precedent for similar centers worldwide. While initially challenged by entertaining these young learners, Maria's ingenuity sparked their interest in problem-solving, learning, and even meal preparation. Drawing upon her extensive observations, she designed innovative learning materials and created a unique classroom atmosphere that allowed children to progress at their own pace. This introduced a newfound sense of freedom in the classroom, as children were empowered to pursue their interests and select their preferred learning materials.

Maria's groundbreaking changes captured the attention of numerous notable figures, educators, and journalists. By 1910, many schools were singing the praises of the "Montessori Method," with academies adopting this approach across Western Europe and beyond. The first Montessori school in the United States opened its doors in Tarrytown, New York, in 1911. Despite her resounding success, Maria Montessori continued to refine her child-centered approach, delivering lectures, writing extensively, and developing teacher training programs to ensure the widespread implementation of her innovative method in classrooms worldwide. Today, the Montessori Method remains a prominent and influential approach to education across the globe.

Explanation of Montessori Philosophy and Principles

Now that I've given you a brief intro on how this revolutionary approach came about, it's time to explain it in more detail since you are interested in implementing it into your parenting approach.

The Montessori method came as a very appealing alternative to the conservative, oppressive education of the 19th century. Maria Montessori was very deliberate in her goal to support children rather than punish them. In addition, she also focused on boosting their innate curiosity and interesting ideas instead of forcing them to memorize factual materials and test their knowledge through a form of interrogation.

In essence, Maria looked at education from a scientific aspect. She believed that the point of schooling children is to shape them into complete persons prepared for all aspects of life. She worked hard to design materials promoting natural, unforced growth and learning. Her techniques and the materials allow children to effortlessly transition toward reading, writing, and mathematics. It creates a learning environment where every skill is gradually developed to merge with every other.

Basically, this method looks at children as individuals eager to learn by nature and hungry to receive knowledge when placed in a supportive learning environment. I can confidently say that this is a very human-like method, as it puts more value on a child's healthy development. You can see it as a holistic approach that aims to nurture and inspire, focusing on every aspect of the individual—physical, emotional, cognitive, and social.

The 'Montessori Philosophy' will give your children a unique opportunity to focus and work on their unique potential rather than submit them to a universal teaching approach. As a result, your little one will grow and shape into a strong and competent individual, a responsible and respectful citizen who appreciates the power of learning and acquiring knowledge.

This child-centered schooling approach is based on careful scientific observations of children from the moment they're born up until they reach adulthood. If you're still skeptical about its success, know that the Montessori approach stood the test of time, as it has been used in different cultures for over 100 years. And the success rate has never disappointed!

Principles of Montessori Education

The basis of Montessori principles is to show respect toward each child's learning process. In fact, they are mainly focused on understanding how children learn, focusing on the nature of attaining knowledge, which is the principal reason that sets Montessori schools apart from all others.

Here are the basic principles of this revolutionary method:

Respect

Since the Montessori philosophy is centered around children, it's only natural to conclude that it stemmed from a deep respect for them as individuals. This means it's all about embracing their uniqueness and the freedom of choice and movement. It allows them to correct their mistakes, leaving them to work at their own pace. If you look at it from a distance, you'll easily see that Montessori educators work with all children with genuine respect toward them.

Individual learning

This learning method is tailored to the needs and interests of every child and is based on their stage of development. The lessons in the materials are presented to each kid individually and are devised based on their academic progress. Montessori teachers are dedicated to tracking their progress and supporting them as they pace through the curriculum.

Holistic approach

Not only is Montessori philosophy based on embracing children's individuality, but it's also focused on educating kids as complete individuals. This means that it considers every aspect of a child's potential, providing stimuli for supporting and developing their intellectual, physical, social, and emotional development. So, apart from encouraging children to delve into the field of language and mathematics, it also drives them to show interest in their cultural and practical lives.

Absorbent mind

As Dr. Montessori determined, the first six years of each child's life are the most important for their growth. She gave an interesting name to this stage, calling it the "absorbent mind." This accurately describes their sponge-like minds, referring to their ability to quickly absorb information from around them (*The Absorbent Mind*, Maria Montessori, 1949). This period is also when kids start to understand the world and their culture, setting the foundation of their personality and intelligence.

Embracing different periods

Being a doctor, Maria Montessori noticed that all children go through different stages as a part of their developmental process. And they don't have the same learning capacity at every stage. In particular, she described those periods when children are most capable of learning new things as 'sensitive periods', describing their capability of memorizing things. The characteristics of these sensitive periods include increased commitment to tasks, improved focus, repetition, and longer periods of concentration.

Freedom

After years of studying and observing children, Dr. Montessori noticed that they learn best when they have complete freedom to move and choose something according to their interests. In the ideal classroom, Montessori students enjoy independence within limits. This means they can move inside the prepared environment, work, and learn where they want, having complete power to decide where they'll focus.

Unique environment

Another interesting thing about Montessori classrooms is the way they look. Those are carefully prepared learning spaces where everything has its place and purpose. Children can often easily notice this sense of order, which helps them form a sense of logical thinking. The main idea is to give them an idea of order in both the environment and their mind. At the same time, it gives them more freedom to follow their interests and improve at their own speed.

Motivation

As I already said, the Montessori approach looks at learning as a reward. They don't give students gold stars or any other kind of reward to motivate them to learn. Instead, children manage to encourage and motivate themselves with their accomplishments after finishing a certain task. This makes them eager to learn more as a way to create a sense of satisfaction by themselves.

Independence

In its essence, the Montessori method focuses on encouraging independence in children. It's all about providing them with the right environment, materials, and guidance to make them think for themselves. According to this philosophy, children are born as avid learners who find it very easy to teach themselves when given a proper push. This is what makes independence one of the ultimate goals of Montessori learning.

Automatic learning

Finally, one of the key principles of this type of learning is the concept of auto-education. This is connected to the previous point that all kids can teach themselves if given the right stimulus. Inspired by this, Montessori learning materials are made to encourage children to discover their abilities and focus their learning on their interests. Teachers do everything they can to make an ideal learning environment for them to educate themselves.

The Importance of Child-Centered Learning in Montessori Learning: Fostering Confidence, Creativity, and Accepting Children for Who They Are

Now that you've already understood that this unique philosophy uniquely treats children, you can see that it differs from what you're used to seeing in the traditional schooling systems. In essence, it all begins with looking at children as equal individuals, not looking down on them as inexperienced little adults—and that approach should be the core of your parenting. The Montessori philosophy states that children must be respected for their identity. This means that you should give them opportunities that will allow them to learn at their own pace, at their own time. At the same time, you should act in a way that would help them feel confident about doing so.

Thanks to her in-depth research, Maria Montessori discovered several interesting things and gained insight into the unique way children learn. This gradually led her to the conclusion that children deserve to be at the center of education. In other words, she advocated that education wasn't something a teacher should do. Instead, she said that everyone should look at learning as a natural process that happens spontaneously.

This child-centered approach promoted that learning doesn't happen when kids listen to words, trying to remember them. It is, in fact, something that naturally comes from experience as the child responds to its environment.

Another thing Dr. Montessori mentions is that you shouldn't try to make a genius out of your child. Instead, you should focus on allowing them to work on their strengths and develop based on their interests. That's the only way your kids can reach their full potential while still being happy and satisfied with their achievements. As a parent, you have to help them when they need it and be at their service, in a way. This will make them build their trust and know that you'll always be there if they need something, knowing they don't have to walk the path alone. However, you should try not to interfere with their way of thinking or give them misleading suggestions. Let them pave their own way, knowing that they can expect your support.

Below, I listed the most notable aspects of Montessori learning as the ultimate child-centered schooling approach:

Foster confidence

At the very core of the Montessori philosophy stands the need to boost children's confidence as they learn. This is a very important thing that the traditional schooling approach often disregards. Thanks to the tailored learning environment that encourages kids to understand what they want, you are helping to pave the way for them to grow into complete individuals who are confident about their capabilities. You can do this by focusing on progress rather than perfection, by recognizing little lessons learned instead of focusing on what needs to be improved next time.

Creativity

Every person has their own creative side. But how well it's developed depends on many factors. In particular, those who were given the freedom to do the things they wanted when they were little turned out to be very imaginative adults. Montessori teaching does this by encouraging students to move in their own direction, embracing their interests. If, for example, your child wants to make up a story some nights instead of reading the whole time, encourage this.

Accept children as they are

The very purpose of this learning is to value every child as a unique and complete individual. This means accepting them as they are and praising their interests and way of gaining knowledge. The Montessori philosophy acknowledges that every child learns uniquely, giving them the freedom to learn and develop as they find suitable. In essence, it lets them go through the curriculum at their own pace under the guidance of their teacher and the custom teaching plan.

The Role of the Teacher in a Montessori Classroom

You're probably wondering exactly why Montessori teachers are different from others and their role. I'm here to try and translate the essence of what this teacher represents by telling you what they do differently.

In essence, the idea of a Montessori teacher greatly differs from the traditional one. You may see these educators as people who offer subtle guidance in the whole education process rather than giving children straightforward instructions. Their job isn't to provide them with factual information but to point them in a certain direction. Additionally, their role is to supply them with all the necessary tools they can use to discover information on their own.

Here are a few things that characterize Montessori teachers and make them stand above the traditional definition:

They encourage independence

To give you an idea of what a Montessori classroom looks like, picture this: instead of seeing one teacher standing upfront and giving a lesson, you'll notice them working with each child separately or with small groups. While doing this, the rest of the children are given complete freedom to work on what interests them.

One of the key roles of every Montessori teacher is to create various structures that will make all students feel independent and confident in their learning abilities. As a parent who wants to achieve this, you need to prepare your classroom-like setting with intention, with the final goal of it being an appropriate and inviting place for your child to learn. Moreover, you're also supposed to slightly change the environment every time your kid shows a change of interest.

They're trained to think like scientists

Every Montessori teacher receives comprehensive training. Montessori certification programs are very demanding; some say they're equal to getting another college degree. This is because they focus on preparing teachers as educators and teach them about other aspects, such as philosophy, art integration, child development, and scientific thinking.

To achieve this in your home environment, observing your child as it learns and grows is the most important thing you need to focus on. It might be useful to keep a notebook when you track their progress, noting what they're most interested in. Write every time you notice a change in how your child approaches something, and observe how extensive their knowledge about particular topics is. This can help you encourage further learning in an area they seem to show extensive interest.

They are focused on long-term goals

Since they don't use a ready-made curriculum, Montessori teachers are creating their own focus on children's long-term progress instead of short-term. You need to allow them to learn at their own pace but also think of additional ways to encourage further learning. Overall, the Montessori approach doesn't evaluate student's progress on a day-to-day basis.

Instead, it allows for a longer period in which they feel free to advance at a speed they feel capable of.

In essence, they're guides

As I mentioned, the key to this approach isn't to train teachers who only tell stories and lectures. Due to the nature of student learning that's encouraged in this way, the teachers are often seen as guides, which is why many call them by that name.

Since this learning is based on the idea of 'freedom within limits', the teacher's primary role is to set those limits without being very obvious. Try to design a well-structured place to give your child a sense of a 'comfort zone'. This will still allow them to expand their knowledge and interests without crossing the set boundaries. If you notice that they're showing interest in something while completely abandoning something else, a simple change in the environment or an honest discussion might be enough to spike their interest.

An Overview of the Montessori Materials and Their Purpose

Even though Montessori learning is an approach that isn't based on universal learning and curriculum, you still need something to follow. Montessori materials are specifically designed for this purpose as hands-on learning tools that can successfully stimulate children's minds and inspire them to learn independently. The most important thing about these is that they succeed in supporting their learning process while at the same time being incredibly easy to use.

Let's see what they are and how they manage to do that!

Montessori materials are focused on teaching one skill at a time, which helps children master certain skills through repetition and practice. It's based on the famous statement of Dr. Montessori that nothing can be engraved in the mind if it doesn't go through the hands first.

These materials are effective because each topic is introduced as a key lesson, inviting students to work on the material independently. After they're done with it, they're supposed to put it back in its allocated place in the classroom. Another important thing you should know about these is that they need to be presented one by one, starting with the easiest and slowly progressing to the hardest. Of course, you must also be intentional and choose the right timing to give them when the child is ready to perceive them.

Here's what a Montessori curriculum is intended to provide:

Hands-on learning

As I said, this approach guides children to discover important learning outcomes through repetition and practice. This is something that proved to be quite effective because it involves both the physical and mental aspects of learning something new.

Error control

The way they're designed, Montessori materials allow children to easily see when they make mistakes and try to fix them. This also encourages their creative thinking as they discover new ways to get something right. Let's give you a simple example—the wooden cylinder won't fit into the square hole, or there will be too many objects left when your child finishes a certain counting activity.

It's all about steady progress

In a well-designed Montessori classroom, the learning materials are arranged in the designated area in left-to-right order, from easiest to hardest. This is a very logical way to place them because it allows children to progress slowly through the curriculum.

Fine motor skills

As I already said, it's all about children getting their hands on things so they can learn and explore. This does wonders for developing their fine motor skills and encouraging concentration and independence, which children will find very useful when they grow up.

One thing at a time

It's always better to learn to remember than to go fast over the material without having the time to reflect on what they learned. This is why the Montessori approach focuses on developing one skill at a time, providing ample space for kids to engage in and practice each.

Auto-instructional

Last but not least, these materials are designed to be used by children on their own, without the parent guiding them. This is the beauty of the Montessori approach, as it allows children to discover and master every skill independently and not rely on someone to constantly give them tips or reassurance.

You need to know that the Montessori Learning materials focus on five key study areas: Practical Life, Sensorial, Mathematics, Language, and Cultural Studies. All of them are designed with the step-by-step approach in mind, allowing children to progress with their learning slowly.

Chapter 2: The Parent's Role in a Montessori Education

As we established, the Montessori philosophy is all about creating a convenient and incredibly suitable environment for students to learn. And your support as a parent is more than welcome here!

Remember that this approach is more of an attitude than a discipline, focusing on life, growth, and development—not only on schooling. It's a great way of initiating a connection between home and school, shifting all the focus to a positive learning experience. So, apart from your role as a careful observer and selfless caregiver, the Montessori approach encourages you to take an active part in your child's activities. This experience acts as a groundwork for sharing knowledge and showing your support while also keeping you up with your kids' interests and achievements.

To each little kid, their family is a unique world. As a parent, you're the first to act as an educator before they even get to go to preschool and learn from others. So, you're there to support and guide your little ones, always encouraging them to keep going forward despite their occasional failures. After all, the process of growing and learning is all about trying to improve yourself and keep going forward no matter the occasional mistakes you make.

Moreover, there are a few other things that you should do as a parent:

- Encourage their creativity
- Remind them to stay organized
- Keep them close to nature
- Let them do things on their own
- Be their model
- Use encouraging words instead of rewards

Ultimately, parents are the ones who lay down the foundation for a thriving learning environment. So, your role in Montessori schooling is to understand your children's needs and interests and stimulate their development. This is the key for your little ones to grow into complete, mature, and self-reliant adults.

The Importance of Observation and Following the Child's Interests in Montessori Education

As with any other type of education, observing students' work and progress is very important. However, when it comes to Montessori education, this is something that you absolutely have to do. Given the nature of this approach, based on leaving children to learn at their own pace and encouraging improvements, observing how they're doing is the only way to see where they're at—development-wise.

As a parent, the opportunity to observe will give you a glimpse into what your child is interested in—or whether they find a certain task more challenging. According to this, you can later decide if they need your gentle guidance or if they're ready to move on to learning something new.

Many parents seem to be amazed by the wide range of opportunities this Montessori philosophy offers. But to be able to follow and evaluate your kids' progress without interrupting this naturally flowing environment, you need to know a few observation rules.

- Please take a seat or silently stand farther away from the active learning setting. Try to make yourself less noticeable and carefully examine your child's behavior.

Focus on their body language and facial expressions as they're doing a certain task. Are they doing something out of boredom or struggling to get the hang of a particular assignment? This is very important to determine so that you know your child's interests and progress level.

- If the child approaches you, please don't try to disrupt their concentration by engaging them in a conversation. Instead, you should gently encourage them to keep up with their work or offer your assistance if they ask for it. If you're observing a larger classroom, simply saying "hello" is enough. Montessori students will know that you just came to observe them, so they won't bother with you.
- Write down everything you notice or have a question about. Don't interrupt the children by speaking up as soon as something comes to your mind. Focus on simply watching and taking notes regarding what you think is worth discussing later.
- Careful observation means you'll need to stay longer; 5 or 10 minutes is not enough to notice everything essential. Tracking your child's progress and discovering their interests takes at least half an hour to an hour.

- If you observe more than one kid, you'll notice they're learning at a different pace, possibly showing interest in different things. And the best thing to do is to follow those interests and try to encourage them. After all, the Montessori approach is about embracing every child's uniqueness and encouraging them to work on their development.

Strategies for Supporting Your Child's Learning at Home via Montessori Principles

Because you wish to provide your child with the best opportunities to learn and develop, I have excellent news for you. Montessori schooling isn't just for a conventional classroom—you can easily use these principles at home!

Whether you're trying to reinforce what your kids are learning at school or pave the way toward discovering their interests—if you like the Montessori philosophy, why not start practicing it now? Here are some things you need to carefully consider to give your kid the ideal Montessori learning experience:

Prepare the environment

One of the principles of this approach is to encourage independence, self-motivation, and order. All Montessori schools have specially designed classrooms that give students freedom, letting them develop a sense of caring for themselves and their surroundings. If you want to turn your home into a productive environment, you need to think about organizing it. First things first, you need to design them in a way that has a designated place for everything your child is going to use. This will also help them easily find something when they need it or put that thing back when they're done. A well-organized environment also offers fewer distractions, so you'll rest assured that your little one will be focused on doing their task.

Make your home look simple

Simplifying your home will help your child better understand what you expect from them. If you're dedicated to giving them full support and constant encouragement, here's a gentle reminder—you can even teach your toddler to return their things to their own place.

If you're looking for practical solutions to this suggestion, I'm here to give you some.

- Limit the toy choice by providing only a few your kid would play with;

- Use open shelves instead of toy boxes so that every item can have its "own place" on the shelf;
- Keep the things your kids use at their eye level;
- Sort items carefully, in boxes or trays, to subtly teach them about order and the importance of keeping everything in place;
- Finally, store some toys away from their reach so you can offer them once they get bored with the ones they're playing with now.

Keep their bedrooms tidy

You should always keep your kids' bedrooms tidy and clutter-free. If the space allows it, try to assign different places for specific activities—a seating area, a self-care area, or a dressing space. In addition, you should also pay attention when choosing the furniture, ensuring that you're buying child-sized items. This will further promote the independence this method strives to achieve, as your child won't feel 'too small' to do the simplest things, like getting dressed or going to bed.

If you have older children, they should feel like they own their little place. The bedrooms should have designated areas for sleeping, playing, and working/studying. This should also be a place that expresses their unique personality or interests, so allow them to hang posters of their favorite bands or include them in the choice of paint color.

Welcome them into the kitchen

If you wish to further reinforce the feeling of independence that Montessori teaching is aimed to provide, one of the best things you can do is make your kitchen an inviting place for your children. Think about placing the groceries on low shelves that your kid can easily reach or place a stool near the counter so they can climb to help you with the dishes or to reach something else. This will eventually make your child feel helpful and more independent at home.

Moreover, you can use child-size silverware and dishware instead of plastic ones that look like a toy. As they grow, you should tailor your home environment to grow with them so they feel just as worthy a contributor as you in doing various home tasks.

Become a Montessori Parent

Being a Montessori parent means that you really have to get into the role of being a supportive and observing caregiver. There are a few qualities of every parent who wishes to incorporate the Montessori principles of schooling at home:

Be observing

I already tackled the power of observation, so I won't make this point long. Overall, you need to take your time and observe your child as they go through their tasks to see their progress and habits. If you notice they're growing a particular interest in something, provide them with materials to explore that area.

Modeling, inviting, and practicing

Ultimately, you should be your child's model as they go through household tasks. You can assist them at the beginning but mainly try to make them look at them as their model. Do the same thing when storing away toys or learning materials. Instead of labeling the shelves to indicate what belongs there, show them by putting away things with them. And don't expect them to get it all right from the first try! Practice makes perfect, and you need to be patient and offer subtle assistance only when needed.

Adapt the environment

The role of your observations is to notice the changes in interests and behavior so that you can modify the learning environment accordingly. If you have older children, include them in the decision-making by giving them options for them to choose from.

Practice life skills

One of the best things that Montessori principles teach is the practice of skills that children will use later in life. The point is to teach children to take care of themselves and their surroundings from a very young age so they can nurture these qualities as they grow into competent adults.

So, include them in the household tasks by letting them dust, wash dishes, put away groceries, prepare meals, etc. You can also let them fold their clothes, match socks, and care for the pet (if you have one).

Explanation of the Montessori Approach to Discipline

Upon researching the Montessori approach, you probably came across some negative comments or stances. Some falsely think this philosophy is about allowing children to do whatever they want, while others claim this approach is very strict. But in reality, the Montessori method falls somewhere in between. In other words, it understands the word 'discipline' based on its root, 'disciple,' which means to 'teach' and 'learn' rather than punish. How should you implement this? Well, next time your child does something wrong, instead of getting angry and punishing them, see it as an opportunity to teach them that's wrong without sounding harsh. Modeling behavior is the most important lesson we can give our children.

You need to present yourself as a nurturer and guide rather than a negative character who thinks of new ways of punishment every time they do something wrong. Here are two aspects you need to take into account in order to approach the topic of discipline the right way:

Feelings versus behaviors

If I am to put it briefly, the Montessori approach teaches that discipline is established keeping inner growth and awareness in mind. This is why it's focused on giving children freedom within well-established limits, so they can get a sense of control themselves, ultimately learning to tell the difference between right and wrong on their own.

As a parent, it's all about focusing on the internal aspects in order to make a positive change without trying to control their behavior. So, instead of getting angry the next time they make a mistake, try to stay calm and don't react. Children, being children, can often do something just because they want to get your attention. That means yelling at them won't help in this situation. You need to gently point out what a negative behavior looks like by reminding them what a positive one looks like. If you notice that they're aggressive, simply explain that such behavior hurts others and redirect them to an activity after you're done explaining. Verbal redirection is a skill to be mastered with time – do your best and keep trying.

Young children often can't understand different types of behavior, especially from other kids. The Montessori approach teaches that all behavior is a form of communication, so you need to act as a translator for them. For example, if you see them trying to take another child's toy, and the other kid pulls away, you can say, "They want to play with it a little more; just wait for them to finish."

Positive reinforcement versus rewards

Another very important thing to remember when it comes to implementing the Montessori approach to discipline is never to use bribes and rewards. I know that you probably think that rewarding your child for something they did right will make a positive impact. However, you're teaching them that every time they do something positive, they should expect a prize. Extrinsic motivation is also one of the worst parent practices, as you teach your child to look to others instead of developing self-discipline.

What you should do, instead, is build intrinsic motivation by giving positive reinforcement. The century-long practice of the Montessori approach has proven that children are most likely to do something if they see an intrinsic value in their work. It's all based on the belief that they should feel pride and pleasure while doing something, as that's longer-lasting than the gold stars and allowance you'd give. So, focus on giving encouragement and appreciation for their effort and well-done job—that's the only way you'll nurture an inner motivation they'll rely on for the rest of their life.

The Importance of Self-Awareness and Self-Care

It's in the roots of the Montessori approach to embrace differences and praise children for who they are. This doesn't only apply to their academic achievements but to their social and emotional levels, as well. So, it encourages children, from a very young age, to care for themselves and be self-aware. And here's why these two things are very important for the child's development:

Self-Awareness

Being a parent and mature adult, you probably know what sets you apart from others, meaning you're self-aware. And if I am to guess, this probably took you quite some time to understand. Children, however, don't have the same experience as you. This is the beauty of the Montessori method—it teaches them to discover more about themselves as they finish tasks, form friendships, and approach problem-solving. It allows them to get to know themselves while being in a safe and incredibly nurturing environment. And as they grow, they'll be able to take this feeling of being aware of who they are and use it to their benefit.

What's so positive about this is that this philosophy teaches kids to accept themselves as they are, not trying to change them in any way. Some things simply make someone who they are, and there's no escape from that. It may be how they work, learn, or approach a certain situation or what they like and dislike. And there's no point in changing these things so the child can "comply" with a particular norm. One of the biggest advantages of the Montessori approach is that it helps them accept themselves and not be ashamed of that. Even though they might face certain challenges, they're still equal contributors to the classroom or social environment as all others. Being aware of their capabilities and difficulties will also make it easier for them to adapt and accommodate them while still being able to show their strengths.

Self-care

Another important thing that this approach teaches students is the notion of self-care. As I've already mentioned several times so far, this is a quality that's nurtured from an early age. So, not only are they taught to take care of their environment and the people that surround them, but they're also encouraged to practice self-care. And that's something that's going to serve them as they grow and shape into adults.

As the Montessori method is all about teaching independence, at the same time, it highlights the importance of caring for themselves. For example, it shows them that they must brush their teeth, wash their hands, and wear clean clothes. Children are encouraged to learn to do these things for themselves so they can be independent and not wait for someone else to do it for them.

Ultimately, the self-care and independence they're taught will help them develop a sense of accomplishment and confidence. It will also teach them that they must dedicate time and focus on their well-being and not neglect themselves.

Involving Grandparents

I'm sure that you, as a parent, have found it thrilling when you learn that you could make an impact and actively participate in the Montessori schooling of your children. But what if I tell you that you can also involve your parents, i.e., the child's grandparents, in the same process? Although you might think this is a 'mission impossible' at the beginning, I'm here to tell you that, with a little work, you can teach them how to contribute to your child's Montessori raising the right way.

The first challenge you might face is that the grandparents might feel hesitant about showing their care differently than they did when raising their children. Or they may find it puzzling as to why they should follow your approach. To help them understand, it's best that you give them real examples and factual information instead of explaining the philosophical principles. And here are a handful of things that might help:

- Instead of helping the baby get up, pause and wait for them to try to do that themselves;
- Don't use baby talk; they will develop and learn to speak faster if you talk to them in a normal voice;

- Instead of spoon-feeding the toddler, teach them to use their hands when eating finger food or try to feed themselves using a spoon or fork;
- Spare your words of praise, and focus on acknowledging their effort;
- Don't use electronic toys or mobile phones to engage them; instead, use different materials or toys that will encourage independent play;
- Don't repeat the word 'no' if they aren't supposed to do something – try to explain why they shouldn't do it so they understand the reasoning behind it;
- Instead of cleaning their mess or toys they scarred all around, involve them in the cleaning process so they'd help.

Dealing with Divorce

All children need to experience a balance between fixed routines and flexibility, no matter the stage of their growth. That being said, most of them find it hard when stressful situations arise, and divorce is one of them. This is an incredibly difficult and turbulent phase that both parents and the child have to go through. If you want to stay consistent with the Montessori philosophy of raising them, you will benefit from using a few strategies that will help them deal with the situation. So, here's what you can do:

Establish order

All children, especially those under 6, are used to functioning in an order. This involves everything they use on a daily basis, from their toys and clothes to their favorite cup or snack. So, the first thing you can do if you're sharing custody with your child's other parent is to try and establish a similar order in your home.

Keep up the routine

It can be really hard to try to keep the same routine between two different places, especially when you know that you have little to no control over the other environment. But both parents need to understand the importance of following a well-established routine so that the child can deal with this unfortunate situation better. So, if they're already used to waking up at the same time, having breakfast, and playing with their toys afterward, don't disrupt it! And if you have to, let them know in advance that there will be a change in their schedule so they'll be prepared.

Give them snuggles

This is something that many kids look forward to, no matter whether they're being dropped off at the kindergarten or by their other parent. So, if they ask for it by leaning forward, give them the extra snuggles they need. Sometimes, you may notice that your kid does the opposite, meaning they want to avoid any physical contact. In this case, be as patient as you can with them.

Chapter 3:
Creating a Montessori Environment at Home

You'd be surprised how many parents have become aware of the benefits of the Montessori schooling approach, realizing its positive effect on their children's growth and development. In addition, Many of them have also become interested in turning the Montessori methods to their benefit and using them to tailor their parenting method to that image.

Because you are reading this book, you are one of those caring parents interested in adapting their home and creating a Montessori environment out of it. However, you're probably wondering which changes you should make to make it an inviting space. Have a look at the information below to ensure that you're considering every aspect of creating a home Montessori setting.

Different Areas in a Montessori Classroom and How to Recreate Them at Home

If you've ever had a chance to see what a Montessori classroom looks like, you've probably noticed that it looks very little like a traditional one. The first difference you'll probably notice is that the instructor doesn't take the front position in the classroom. Instead, children are allowed to freely explore the space, choosing which activities they'd like to do. And if you liked the idea of not always being responsible for giving them instructions, you're probably interested in implementing the Montessori method at home. Here's what you should focus on:

Simplify your home

The first thing you need to consider is simplifying your home. This means you need to modify it to fit your child's age but without incorporating things they don't need. For example, if your little one is still a baby, they won't need much to start their Montessori journey. You only have to place a few things in their sleeping or play area to keep them satisfied. However, you still shouldn't forget to childproof your home once they start to walk. Keep sharp objects out of their reach, use wooden baby gates to limit their walking, and cover all electrical outlets. As they slowly grow up, you'll need to give them separate spaces in your home that they can use without limitations, but by then, they'll know how to care for and value them.

Create child-friendly spots

The Montessori philosophy encourages children to be more independent. And if you want to promote this quality at home, you need to think about the different ways to make it more accessible for them. One of the first areas you should start from is the kitchen; place a few shelves on their eye level, buy child-sized cutlery and dishware, and, of course, an appropriate chair for their age. This will help them become directly involved in the food preparation process and even make their own meals.

Put most of their toys away

No matter whether you're guided by the saying 'less is more,' the Montessori approach states that having fewer toys is better for children. Why? Because you'll have more to give once they become tired of those they currently play with. If you give all of them at once, they go through their options quickly, and you'll end up buying more and more toys. Another useful tip is to ditch the bottomless toy boxes and display the toys on shelves. If your child is at an appropriate age, you can also talk to them about waste and unnecessary buying so they'd understand they don't need every toy from the store's shelves to keep themselves entertained.

Adapt your entryway

Making small changes to your entrance area can have a huge impact when making your home Montessori-friendly. Think about adding hooks or a shoe rack corresponding to their height so they have everything at reach. You can also hang a small mirror at their height so they can see themselves as they're preparing. This will help you stay calm on those rushed mornings, as your kids will be able to put on their coats and shoes without waiting for your assistance. Moreover, it'll also help build their sense of responsibility and independence from a young age.

Keep things at easy-to-reach places

Just like their toys and groceries, you must consider putting everything your child uses in an easily accessible place. This means that their clothes, hygiene items, shoes, books, and whatever else they use should be put in an easy-to-reach location. This is a great way of promoting independence because they'd be able to do much more on their own without calling for you every time they need something.

Keep the color scheme and decor minimal and natural

For whatever reason, many parents think that the children's rooms should be painted in bright colors. But the truth is, they'll function much better in a calming, naturally-painted environment. So, there's no need to waste lots of time and resources to change how your home looks. Instead, you can easily paint the walls with a neutral color, try to buy more wood, glass, metal, or other natural materials instead of plastic, and use framed art to decorate your walls.

The Importance of Order and Simplicity in a Montessori Environment

At its very core, the Montessori method is all about creating order and valuing the simple look of an environment. All Montessorians believe that the student, teacher, and environment should work in harmony to achieve the best results. Therefore, you should pay equal attention to keeping a tidy and highly functional space for your child to learn and thrive in.

Even as an adult, you probably feel much better when your home is clean and tidy and everything is put in its place. So, you can already see why creating a simple and well-arranged Montessori space for your little one is so important.

Montessori teachers believe that when the learning environment is set up appropriately, the child will find it easier to develop independence, concentration, and coordination. This is also a great way to subtly introduce the sense of order and how every place they attend in the future should be organized in a particular manner. As Montessori instructors do their best to prepare the classroom environment, you should do the same for your home space. Every single element of the environment should have its own designated place. This will teach children where to find a particular item they're looking for and where they should put it when it's not in use. This creates a sense of order on an intuitive level, making it easy for them to navigate the space and tidy up after they're done with each activity.

To help your child maintain the sense of order they have in the classroom or create the same feeling at home, you have to look at simplicity as your point of orientation. This means that you should let the idea of keeping things simple and organized guide you as you reconfigure your environment to create a Montessori environment. This will inspire your child's curiosity, keep them concentrated while doing an activity, and bring them a sense of calm and familiarity.

Here's what you can do to achieve this:

Remember that 'less is more'

Although it may sound surprising to you at first, it's proven that children show more appreciation when they have fewer things around them. You can easily put this to the test by storing away around half of their toys. You'll easily notice that they now appear more interested in playing with the ones they have. They'll also find it easier to pick the ones they like off the sleeves.

Learn to let go

Another important tip that will help keep your home simple and in order is to toss all the things your child doesn't use. This means you should practice throwing away broken toys you can't fix or donate gently used items once your kid outgrows them. It's a great tip to keep a tidy and clutter-free environment!

Rotate

As I've already mentioned before, the point of storing away half of your child's possessions is to rotate between them. This will keep the environment engaging and introduce a variety. A good thing to remember is to rotate the toys every few weeks to keep them interested in using what they have. You can easily determine when it's the time to switch by observing their behavior. Once you notice that they're getting bored with a certain toy or activity, make a change!

Focus on aesthetics and order

Finally, your home needs to look appealing. It should not be overly simple to the point of giving the sense of being empty. So, use the toys and decor you decided to keep and position them to make the space seem enticing and in order. You can rest assured that you'll get a positive response from your child to this humble sense of order. Removing clutter is good for your child's mind and yours. This, however, can be a daunting task. I recommend doing one shelf or drawer at a time. One per day, or one per week, whatever your schedule allows, to chip away at your goal without making it an added cause of stress.

How to Adapt Your Home to a Montessori Environment Room by Room

There are many reasons why, as a parent, you should adapt your home to the Montessori standards and make it a thriving space for your child. And the biggest one is, perhaps, because it will help them develop the ability to learn about their surroundings through meaningful play. The easiest way to implement the Montessori principles in your home environment is by focusing on one room at a time. Take simple steps to adapt to it, little by little, so you don't feel overwhelmed by the job. After all, you probably won't have to make as many changes as you initially thought!

But before I give you straightforward tips about turning every corner into a Montessori-friendly space, here's why you need to make the environment as organized as you can:

- You need a designated place for everything because it will help your child learn where everything goes more quickly. This is the main Montessori principle you need to follow if you wish to teach them to be more responsible and tidy up after themselves.
- To make your rearrangement successful, remember that everything should be easily accessible for your children. This will not only give a sense of order, but it will also make your child more independent. They'll be able to reach for almost everything they need without asking for your help!

Here are a few ideas of how you can create an intuitive environment, room by room:

Kitchen

I think that it would be easier for you to start by adapting your kitchen space. At the same time, this area offers probably the most opportunities for encouraging independence as your little ones grow. From engaging them to help put away the groceries to cleaning up the work area or table after they finish a meal, there are plenty of ways to turn your kitchen into a Montessori environment.

As I mentioned, you need to make all the changes, keeping in mind that your kids need to easily reach everything. So, here's how you can turn this project of yours into a successful outcome:

- **Step stools**: place a step stool to make it easier for your child to reach the sink and wash their hands, help you while preparing meals, or wipe the dishes. You can use the same tip for your bathroom and place a stool they can climb onto to brush their teeth or wash their face in the morning.
- **Tables and chairs**: if you can, purchase a child-size table and chair so they'll have their own special place in the kitchen. This will make them feel like they truly belong to that area, making as large a contribution as

any other member of your family. These will provide them with a comfortable place to eat and prepare meals. You can also use this space to teach them the responsibility of cleaning up after themselves and keeping the eating area spotless.

- **Utensils**: this is yet another thing I briefly mentioned before—you need to provide your kid with child-sized eating utensils. This includes everything from spoons and forks to dishes, bowls, plates, and cups. Moreover, you should also remember to buy real cutlery, not plastic ones, as the first will teach them how to use them and behave properly at the table.

- **Food and drinks storage:** you cannot easily replace your fridge and buy a smaller one, but you can reorder it to make it child-friendly. How, you ask? Well, it's much simpler than you may think. Focus on storing the healthy snacks on the lowest shelves in the refrigerator or pantry so your kid can easily reach them. In addition, keep their favorite beverages in small pitchers down in the fridge—you can also place child-sized cups nearby. Whenever your child asks for water or juice, let them help themselves. They might indeed make a mess the first couple of times, but it's nothing that a sponge or a napkin won't clean.

Bedroom

Next comes the bedroom, and you'll probably have fun rearranging the stuff here to create an inviting Montessori environment. After all, your kid's bedroom should also be where they'll do their homework, play, relax, and get dressed. So, you must arrange it in a way so that everything is in its own place—no clutter and no distractions.

Similar to how you'll organize your kitchen, your child's bedroom should also be very accessible for them. Here's how you can do that:

- **Storage**: gather all their toys, games, or other interactive materials and place them on low shelves, making it easy for your kid to get them. You can also consider separating them into various baskets by category so they can find an item based on what they're interested in playing with.
- **Clothing:** store the clothes they use daily in the lower drawers or storage bins/ baskets. Don't forget to keep these at their eye level so your child can easily spot them. If you have younger children who still

can't tell between seasonal clothing, you should arrange the drawers they get easy access to with appropriate clothes for the season. This will avoid situations like them wanting to wear a winter coat in summer, and you won't have to interfere with their decision.

- **Bedding**: for smaller kids, you should opt for a floor bed so they can easily jump to and from without your help—or the possibility of hurting themselves. This will also make it easy for them to make the bed after they wake up.
- **Decorations**: it's best to ask for your kid's opinion when deciding what type of decor to buy for their room. And if you're going shopping on your own, please keep in mind their personal preferences. So, if they're interested in dinosaurs, don't make their room resemble a cosmic theme. Another good tip to use is to include a mirror in the room, especially if your child is a little older. This will make it easier for them to select outfits by trying different combinations and seeing what they like best.
- **Paint**: Another good idea is to ask them about their paint preferences when it comes to their room. If

you're worried that they'll make a choice they won't like after a short time, give them a few options they can choose from and with which you feel comfortable.

Living room

I'm going to finish this list with the living room as the last piece you should adapt to align with the Montessori principles. So, what you need to know before you start making any changes is that you should approach it similar to how you did with the bedroom. However, the living room is where all your family spends their free time, so you can't transform it entirely. Here's what you can do:

- **Furniture:** if your child has a habit of moving the furniture in their room, they might try to do the same in the living room. If you don't want this to happen, you'll need to set some boundaries—allow them to move only certain pieces or nothing at all.
- **Shelving**: similar to what you'll do with the other rooms, make sure to add at least a few shelves that would be easy to access. You can use them to place your kid's puzzles, books, flashcards, or other toys they use while playing in the living room. Again, everything should have its designated place so the

child would know where to return it once they're done using it.

- **Floor mats**: just as you put the child-sized table in the kitchen, you can use a colorful floor mat to let them know where they're supposed to play. A good tip to follow is to choose one that's easy to roll up and store away after playtime. The same rule stays for their living room toys, as well: rotate them occasionally to keep them interesting for a longer time so that you don't end up needing to buy new ones every month or two.

Chapter 4: Montessori Principles and Activities for Infants (months 1-12)

As a parent, you might wonder when to start implementing the Montessori approach to raising your child. And the answer is—you can do it from as early as when they're still infants. But to understand why you need to abide by the Montessori principles from your child's birth, you need to let go of every conventional attitude you have toward education. After all, this is not a conventional schooling model because it views learning as something that needs to be intertwined with living. It's a holistic approach that helps children realize their full potential, so why not start paving that way from the earliest age?

Addressing the Developmental Needs and Milestones of Infants in a Montessori Way

After decades of careful observation and research, biologists have determined some theories about how children develop cognitively. According to a famous biologist and psychologist, Jean Piaget, children are naturally curious beings eager to explore their surroundings. (*The Language and Thought of the* Child, Jean Piaget, 1923) This is especially true for the little ones, as they experiment, discover, and build their knowledge as they move around or get in touch with different items or people.

Here's what's important that you know for the development and biology of infants.

Developmental needs and biology

To make it easier to understand the babies' needs and capabilities, you need to know the basic human tendencies Dr. Montessori introduced. Those are the natural drives or basic needs that every human being has. But what you probably aren't aware of is that babies are actually capable of experiencing quite some things from birth. Some of the things every individual experiences in the infant stage are associating with other people, orientating, exploring, communicating, etc. This means that babies in their infant stage are biologically wired to adapt to the environment in which they're placed. How do they do this? By acting upon the drives I just mentioned, they help them make sense of the world.

However, Montessori introduced two other abilities that weren't addressed by then, and that's the notion of the Absorbent Mind and Sensitive Periods. Just as a quick reminder of these things I already spoke about, the Absorbent Mind is a time-sensitive period during which they enjoy the greatest capacity to learn. On the other hand, Sensitive Periods refer to times of intense interest in learning different skills (language, movement, order, etc.). So, this is what you can do to address their needs during the infant stage:

Create their first prepared environment

The purpose of the so-called 'prepared environment' is to give the child enough space to feel connected and capable of doing things. So, your infant's first such setting should be designed in a manner to help them explore, orient, and act on their drives. And it's not impossible to achieve this aim even without materialistic items. Here's how it should look:

- It should be safe and accessible.
- It should have structure and order.
- Age-appropriate.
- Interesting, showing elements from the real world.

Montessori nursery

Instead of creating a place oriented around the parents, the Montessori one needs to be designed around the infant. For example, many parents choose an open floor space rather than including adult-size furniture. Instead of a crib, they opt for a floor bed. Here's what it contains in addition to this:

- Calm, muted-colored walls
- Low-hung wall art
- Rug or play mat
- Low mirror

Freedom to move

Children are born with the desire to move, and as a parent, you need to provide them with the ideal environment for that. Although their motor skills will develop naturally, they would benefit if you give them an unrestrictive environment that will help them gain strength. Instead of placing your baby in something that restrains their movement, such as a jumper, you need to put it into an open but defined movement area. There, they can choose how and where to move and explore, all within the safe limits you've set.

Clothing

Instead of swaddling the baby down, offering them the same freedom of movement they had in the womb is better. Therefore, during their motor development, opt for practical and properly fitting outfits so they won't cause any frustration.

Baby registry

Naturally, you can guess that a Montessori registry will look different from what you're used to seeing. This one should contain a topponcino (thin flat security pillow), an area for free movement, mobiles, and other carefully chosen toys. When choosing them, remember that they need to offer active entertainment, work on an isolated sensory experience, are realistic, and are made from natural materials (wood, metal).

Milestones

You need to be aware of several important infant milestones, which will be helpful for both you and your infant as they grow and develop. I will divide them into three periods, each based on the different areas of children's development. (American Academy of Pediatrics)

0-3 months

This is when the child sleeps for about ⅔ of the day. Apart from the crying and fussiness and predominantly automated movements, here's what happens during this period:

- Babies are active listeners to suns and voices
- Cry for assistance
- Coordinate eye movements
- Becomes acquainted with their hands and feet

During this time, you can offer high-contrast imagery, don't interrupt their increased concentration, and slow down your daily movements so they can observe you.

3-6 months

You'll notice that your baby will start moving more, with intent and coordination. They might also show more interest in colors and patterns. This is also when infants start to grab and hold onto objects, so you can provide them with different toys to practice these movements, such as rattles or grasping beads.

6-9 months

This is the prime time of their sensorial learning, so infants start to sit unassisted, see better, and develop their fine motorics. During the end of this stage, they begin using their fingers more precisely and know how to imitate certain actions.

To support this stage of development, you can introduce more engaging toys, provide pull-up support, or even let them try to drink from a cup.

9-12 months

You'll start to notice how more independent your baby is getting as they develop their mobility. At this point, most infants can crawl, stand, or even take their first steps. They will also learn several gestures, like clapping, pointing, and waving.

The most important thing to do during this phase is to baby-proof your home. The odds are that they'll start going out of their movement area, so make sure to create an overall safe space. However, be wary not to make their environment over-stimulating now that they can easily reach more things.

Respecting Emotions, Setting Limits, and Discipline in the Infant Years

If you are to set a proper basis for your child's development, you have to do it practically from the moment they're born. But this doesn't only include buying suitable toys or re-making your home. You need to pay attention to other things, such as acknowledging their emotions, setting reasonable limits, and introducing discipline.

Emotional Development in Infants

When speaking of infants and emotions, it's safe to say that those are the first spontaneous expressions they develop. From a practical viewpoint, they navigate parents' behavior and help establish a solid relationship between the baby and their surroundings. Truth be told, the emotions you show toward your child in their earliest stage of development will greatly influence how they adapt and grow in the environment. In addition, the level of closeness they establish with you will affect their personality.

It's very important that you don't act with rejection toward them to help them develop a sense of worth and security. It's been proven that if infants are treated with love and respect, they grow to feel more confident in themselves. So, you must act upon their individual tempo and create an environment that will allow complete freedom.

In essence, you should develop activities that will keep them enthusiastic and help structure their personality in the future. Children love it when they're involved in activities that satisfy their inner needs and emotions. To encourage them, you can use musical play, puppets, or other simple instruments to help them release their emotions.

Is Setting Limits too Early for an Infant?

It is never too early to start with limits. This is essential based on the Montessori philosophy, so let's discover its unique approach. Once your infant starts to move more and becomes interested in exploring the surroundings, it's time to employ some restrictions—but not in a conventional way. For example, the best course of action is to remove any items from your home that you don't want your baby to touch. After all, it's your job to create a prepared environment that would be safe for them to explore without putting restrictions.

There are some things you can't possibly remove or hide. If you have older children, they might need some of their items to be kept in a certain place that your infant can easily crawl to. Think about storing these things differently or putting a shelf in another place. Sometimes, even putting an item from the self into the drawer beneath can be a successful way to solve this issue.

The limits you have to set in the environment are about balancing freedom and social expectations. Always try to place limitations in the most natural way possible while your baby still has enough freedom to make their exploring trips.

Here are a few other things when it comes to setting limits for your infant in your home:

- **Model**: Children, especially the little ones, act like sponges in absorbing your behavior. So, the best way to set limits is to stop doing something you don't want your infant to mimic. Or, if you want to teach them how to get something right, set an example by doing that exact thing in front of them.
- **Redirect**: If you can't move something to a different place, you can try redirecting your baby away. You can do this by simply saying that it has to stay there and inviting them to do some other activity, like playing with their toys.

- **Verbal cue**: Instead of repeatedly saying "no," you can say "stop" when you see they're doing something potentially dangerous.

Preschoolers and the Montessori Notion of Discipline

As I already said in one of the previous chapters, Montessori parenting will teach you that the notion of discipline is quite different from the traditional one you're used to. In other words, it isn't a way to restrict your child or take something away, but rather teaching them what to do instead by illustrating the consequences.

However, you're probably aware that your infant won't be able to respond to discipline the same way your older child will. So, you need to develop a gentler approach that will show results. The most important thing to do during this development stage is to observe their actions closely. Although they can't use words to let you know how they feel or what they want, they're still little people, so you need to try and figure this out on your own. After a while, you'll find it easier to understand what a particular way of crying or a grimace means.

Instead of punishing or yelling at them when they scream at the top of their lungs or do something they're not supposed to do, try to stay calm and redirect their attention. Distraction is a useful technique at this age. You should also act as their model and not yell in front of them.

Even though infants cannot possibly respond to discipline, they can react to unconditional love.

To help you better understand how developing inner discipline works in real life, here are a few tips you can try:

- Use clear language to explain the consequences of a certain action. Of course, you can only do this during the end of the infant stage when they can understand better what you're talking about. If possible, also try to illustrate what can happen if they do something they shouldn't.
- Allow for freedom but within a range of choices. This applies to the environment you've created and how they should act in it. Use simple language and modeling to guide them toward doing the right actions.
- Validate your little one's emotions by showing interest and trying to respond to their behavior. Keep calm and show them you're doing your best to understand and answer their needs. This is the best

way to prevent destructive behavior as they grow older.

Suggestions of Montessori Practical Life Activities, Sensorial Materials, Language Activities, Mathematics Materials, and Cultural Activities for Infants

Although you may seem surprised, the truth is Montessori principles and study materials can be applicable even to infants. In fact, the sooner you implement this into your child's life, the better they'll be at thriving independently and responsibly. It's important to start closely monitoring and supporting your baby's needs from the youngest age and offer them proper stimulation and positive challenges to promote their autonomy and boost their learning skills.

There are several aspects you can focus on while your child is still in their infant stage of development, and they are:

Practical life activities

These activities are meant to teach the child how to respond to the real-world environment. And that's undoubtedly what the Montessori method aims to achieve—teach children in the sphere of education and things related to their everyday practical life. These activities include movement, such as eating, drinking water, or holding things. It's all done to help them get a sense of each movement and refine it. In addition, these involve gaining a sense of coordination, order, and independence. Putting things in a specific location so they know where they'll find them when they need it helps them develop a notion of both order and coordination. In addition, the Montessori method suggests providing them with simple toys or other items that should make them use their cognitive ability, which will help them improve their concentration.

Sensory activities

According to the Montessori philosophy, sensorial activities exercise the five senses of infants—visual, auditory, olfactory, tactile, and gustatory. As children become incredibly receptive to developing this at the end of their infant stage, you should focus on providing them with as many sensorial experiences as possible. These will teach them to understand similarities vs. differences—to compare different objects and decide.

Here are a few activities based on the Montessori method that you can use:

- Design a "Treasure Basket" and put different toys and items inside so they can explore what's in there. You can also present them with different musical instruments they can use and explore the sounds they make

- Water play: place a few water-resistant items into a bucket with water and let them try and catch them.
- You can also help them get familiar with different shapes and materials by creating sensory baskets. You can put various wooden elements or wood pieces or create a summer basket with a bunch of seashells in different shapes. These are bound to keep them engaged for quite some time!

Language activities

Montessori-suitable language activities assist infants in exploring the relationship between different sounds and symbols. They do this through the use of movable alphabet letters, cards, or objects. Why are they important? Because they help prepare them for reading and writing.

The learning activities need to involve several of their senses, meaning they're usually auditory, visual, and kinesthetic. Here are a couple of Montessori language activities you can practice with your little one:

- **Talking, but not using 'baby talk'**- It's believed that using 'baby talk' can negatively impact your child to the point of 'dumbing it down.' This means that you should avoid that kind of language and speak to them as you would to an older child. This will train them to understand your words better and faster.

- **Reading or singing** are important activities to do with your baby. Reading will not only help to develop their language abilities sooner, but it can also help them to develop a love for books that will last even when they grow up. On the other hand, singing will help you introduce your child to rhythm, rhyming, and creative expression of emotions from an early age.

Math activities

Dr. Montessori noticed that a sense of mathematical thinking emerges as early as when the children are still infants, which is why she encourages different activities to be included. Knowing that the youngest children learn through movements and exploration, you need to prepare the environment in a way that offers appropriate stimulation and feedback. The best way to plant the notion of math into their minds is by using different items that will show them the cause-effect occurrence. So, instead of battery toys, bouncy chairs, and flashing lights, your infant should be allowed to explore different shapes and objects, how materials fill certain spaces, or how not every item lands or weighs the same.

So, when applying the Montessori method, you can start using comparative language, such as "smaller," "bigger," "lighter," "heavier," etc. You can also mention the shape of a certain item they're playing with, such as the round ball, square block, etc.

Cultural activities

The cultural activities in a Montessori environment expose kids, for the first time, to several areas of knowledge they'll naturally come across later in life. So, these activities aim to provoke their interest in the world sooner, including many aspects, such as history and culture, people, art, music, etc.

The Montessori philosophy suggests that the easiest activity you can do—once they start sitting and interested in playing—is to purchase a globe. You can even look for a child-friendly one that has different colors so that it would be visually appealing. They can play with it by spinning and looking at the different shades, and you can maybe point to a specific area and talk about what it's famous for.

Chapter 5:
Montessori Principles and Activities for Toddlers (ages 1-2)

Once your child reaches the age of one, you'll notice their ability to use their hands has increased. Usually, they stop crawling and begin walking around during this period, so their hands are free to use. Naturally, you'll want to have your home environment childproofed and make sure that no sharp objects come in their way. Moreover, children between the ages of one and two show an increased sense of curiosity, and you'll find them climbing onto things as they're challenging their gross motor skills.

You should be aware of a few things if you're interested in applying Montessori principles to support their development process, from attending to their growing demands and introducing discipline to engaging in various activities that will promote their healthy development.

Addressing the Developmental Needs and Milestones of Toddlers in a Montessori Way

So, to be able to create the ideal Montessori environment for your child to grow in, you need to be fully aware of their time-sensitive needs and milestones. Here's what you should keep in mind:

Developmental Needs and Biology

Generally speaking, toddlers' needs involve learning how to use their hands differently. So, you'll see them working on their grip, doing a hand-to-hand transfer, holding and carrying objects around the house, or trying to reach something farther away. As I mentioned, this is also when they begin to climb onto things, both because they're trying to get a hold of something or simply to test their newly discovered ability. Apart from practicing their motor skills, they'll also start experimenting with self-expression and communication.

Your toddler will already have some experience practicing their movement and developing a sense of order by now. Now, you'll notice that they're becoming quite interested in examining and playing with small objects. As parents, your job is to keep all choking hazards out of their reach while still giving them enough opportunities to explore safely and satisfy their needs. If you're wondering why they have such an insatiable interest, it's because of the extremely sensitive period they're going through. This is a very important step in their growth process because it develops fine motor skills and a better grip. These are essential for future movements and future activities, including writing.

Another important aspect toddlers show interest in is language and vocabulary; since this is when they start to actively work on their communication and self-expression skills, it's only natural that they'll be interested in learning new words. A key thing to remember is that, as a parent, you're helping your child develop their brain as much as you communicate and interact with them. The development of language centers is very time-sensitive, and it's almost impossible to help them fully mature if you don't give your child proper stimulation.

Overall, you need to be fully aware of their needs as they grow up so that you'll be able to properly address them. Given the nature of your toddler's development and their time-sensitive needs, you must act timely and with the right Montessori principles to ensure optimal stimulation and growth.

Milestones

Similar to knowing their needs, you also need to be aware of the cognitive milestones of children between the ages of one and two. This is all about the changes in their brains that happen around a certain time. So, apart from discovering how to use different objects and learning about symbolic play, here are a few important milestones you need to be aware of:

Toileting

This doesn't have to be the horrible process that many parents perceive it to be. Just as with any other activity your child tries to master, there will also be trial and error with this one. Children pick up attitudes from grown-ups, especially their parents because they spend most of their time with them. Instead of screwing up your face when they miss the toilet and pee on the floor, give your best to act supportive so they'd get it right next time.

During this process, closely follow your toddler's behavior to see how they improve over time. Does putting a portable potty in every room work best, or do they prefer to use the toilet seat in the bathroom? From being clumsy at the beginning to slowly building skills around using the toilet, closely follow them during the process until they master it.

This is not a toilet training book, but I would suggest starting sooner rather than later. You will have to deal with many accidents, but you will be surprised how your child can rise to the occasion and quickly learn toileting skills.

New siblings

One of the trickiest things to deal with as your child is at this age is welcoming a new baby or having an older kid trying to boss them around. So, one of the ways to prepare your toddler for the arrival of the new baby is to try to illustrate what life with them would look like. For example, you can include it in preparing the environment for your new family member, encourage them to talk to them while they're still in the belly, and keep the environment simple.

It's very important not to cause them to feel neglected; maybe you can ask for someone's help with the new baby so that you have more time to spend with your toddler or involve them in the caring process from time to time. Moreover, spend enough time with each child and engage in creative activities—alone or together.

Getting rid of pacifiers

For some toddlers, this is one of the hardest milestones to reach, as not all of them feel the same connection to it. If you've been using the Montessori approach from the start, you didn't even use pacifiers that much. The first step in helping your little one phase out from their use is to let them use it only for sleeping. Keep the pacifier away for the rest of the day so they don't feel tempted to use it. And if they are repeatedly asking for it, try to get to the root of the problem; maybe they need something to engage with using their hands or are seeking a connection. Therefore, test out alternatives to see whether they need something else to take their mind off the pacifier.

Other notable milestones

- Identifying family members in pictures
- Starts solving simple problems
- Enjoys cause-and-effect relationships
- Enjoys treasure-hunts
- Answers to simple directions
- Uses exploring to learn
- Can choose between alternatives

Respecting Emotions, Setting Limits, and Discipline in the Toddler Years

Since your child experiences the greatest development during their first years, it's only natural to assume that this is when you must take great care. If you're interested in creating a Montessori home environment to help them thrive, you need to know what to consider to help them make the most out of it. Here are a few things to pay attention to:

Consider and Always Respect Their Emotions

This doesn't only mean that you need to be aware of and address them; it also means that you should offer proper guidance to help regulate them. Your toddler's emotions aren't something to disregard or stay indifferent to. No matter how pointless their reactions might seem at certain times, remember that they result from children's inner emotions. So, the least you can do is to show respect and try to address them.

An important thing to keep in mind is that almost every time your little one presents strong emotions, the outcome depends on your reaction. It's been proven that their emotional experiences at the youngest of age stay deeply engraved into their brains, meaning they'll influence their behavior as they grow up. (John Bowlby, Mary Ainsworth, Daniel J. Siegel) Look for ways to calm your toddler down whenever they have an emotional outburst, as this is how you leave a favorable impression. A simple hug can work wonders. Distraction still works at this age – humor or comforting songs can go a long way.

Define the Most Essential Limits for Your Toddler

The best thriving environment for toddlers is when they grow in order and predictability. Having consistent routines and reasonable expectations means that they're getting optimal rest, nutrition, and engagement. In addition, you need to set ground rules around which they'll function. Think about what's essential for them and your whole family, and set up an environment that makes it easier to follow those rules. For example, the only place to eat is on the table, playing is allowed in certain areas only, and so on.

Know that it's okay to set limits, as those are what will make it easier to keep them safe and show them how to be respectful. And no matter how hard it sometimes gets to set those, always remember that well-thought-of limits will help your toddler shape and grow into a responsible adult. And the best time to start practicing this is when they're still little and actively developing.

A good rule of thumb is to be as clear with your limits as possible. Toddlers need to know what they can expect. However, be wary not to set too many rules and create a feeling that they're growing up in a strict environment. Stick to placing a few simple and clear ones so they'll know their limits and form their behavior around them.

Here are a few guidelines to follow when setting the limits for your toddler:

- Make them logical and age-appropriate
- Express them clearly
- Don't explain them all the time
- The first limits you set should be regarded to your toddler's safety

Disciplining Your Toddler

As I mentioned before, the Montessori approach looks at the notion of discipline quite differently than the traditional idea of it. If you are to raise your child following its principles, your home shouldn't have a place for bribes, threats, or punishments. All those are extrinsic motivations that don't result in a long-term effect. And your child will only cooperate with you to escape punishment or to get a 'well-done' sticker.

Each time your toddler challenges you, try to look at the situation as a teaching opportunity for you and a learning one for them. The main idea of introducing discipline in your home is to provoke cooperation between you and your child. And this is how you can achieve that:

- Involve your toddler in the situation
- Try problem-solving together
- Make sure to manage expectations
- Talk in a way that will make them listen to you

Of course, all these must be age-appropriate; find a way to talk or explain something that will be easy for them to understand. Moreover, you should also find a way to work with them so they'll still feel like they have some control over the situation. A simple question, "How can we solve this problem?" is enough to make them stop for a moment and actively engage in the process of finding a solution.

So, try to understand their impulses as the main reason for their sudden outbursts and address them. Moreover, try to devise a solution that involves teaching rather than punishment. Be a role model for your toddler and make them look upon you as an example of how they should behave. This is the ultimate recipe for establishing good discipline in your household without taking drastic and ineffective measures.

Focus on Developing Skills

When your little one is a toddler, it's important to focus on developing a few skills that will serve them even later as they grow into responsible adults. These include:

Sharing

During their infant stage, your child probably didn't object when you took something out of their hand. However, these things often change once they grow a bit and enter their toddler stage. Now that they've developed a sense of self, you may see them hold onto their toys, unwilling to share them with other kids. This is why it's very important to teach them to share, and here are a few things you can try out:

- Instead of asking your toddler to share an item with another kid, teach them to share by taking turns. Let them use it for as long as they want while the other child patiently waits for their turn.

- In public playgrounds, it can be more difficult to set this into practice. If you notice another child waiting to use the swing, you can tell them you're aware of that by saying that you see they'd want a turn and that the swing will be available soon. And to your child, you can point out that someone else likes to swing so they can count to ten before their turn.

No biting!

Now that their teeth are out, you might notice they sometimes use them to bite you or another child/adult. As this is no behavior you should tolerate, you should address it as soon as you notice it.

When angry, acknowledge their feelings by saying you can see their anger, but you can't allow them to bite you. Give them time to calm down and check up with the other kids to see if they're okay. Know that this stage may require patience and repetition with your toddler, but remember not to take their behavior personally.

Dealing with tantrums

Usually, toddlers have tantrums when something doesn't go their way. No matter the cause, the first thing you need to do is try to calm them down. No reasoning or explanation will help when they're in the middle of this 'episode,' so allow them to settle before you take any action. You can try offering them a cuddle, acknowledging that it's okay for them to feel angry, and not interrupting them while expressing their feelings. However, this doesn't mean that you should ignore their tantrums. Be patient until they pass so you can offer a solution and make amends afterward.

Suggestions of Montessori Practical Life Activities, Sensorial Materials, Language Activities, Mathematics Materials, and Cultural Activities for Toddlers

As I've mentioned, you must closely monitor, care, and support your child's needs. Knowing that they vary depending on the developmental stage, you must engage them with different activities supporting their growth. Here are a few that answer different aspects of their development during their toddler phase:

Practical Life Activities

Remember that every child is different; not all will respond with the same interest and enthusiasm to the same exercises. Of course, some practical life activities based on the

Montessori method that you can try and are toddler-appropriate include the following:

- Involve your toddler in the meal prep process by giving simple tasks to work on, such as ripping herbs, transferring food, or stirring
- Let them practice self-care, such as brushing their hair, washing their teeth or hands, or choosing their clothes
- Let them help you around the house by putting things back into their place, watering the plants, or brushing a pet

Sensory Activities

- Consider their capability level when thinking about which sensorial practices you can incorporate. Don't let your toddler do something very complicated to avoid frustration and anger episodes. For example, toddlers are often interested in exploring the environment through colors, taste, smell, or sounds, so be guided by these. Here are a few sensory activities that are aligned with the Montessori philosophy:

- You can create a DIY activity called Smelling Bottles by giving them a sniff of different foods/ aromas. You can help them pair the scent with real-life food and enjoy it as they explore the connection.
- Another good activity to develop their sound sensitivity is making Sound Bottles. All you need is a few cardboard boxes and objects you'll place inside. Create a pair out of which sound, meaning you'll put the same item in two boxes. Start with three pairs (six boxes), let your toddler shake them, and connect the pairs that sound the same.

Language Activities

Now that they've begun engaging in conversations more, you might wonder how you can help them develop this ability better. A few things you need to remember when thinking of activities that engage your toddler's language activity is that you need to start with a good foundation. The Montessori method implies focusing on speaking and listening first and engaging them by reading stories or singing songs. Keep the learning process concrete by using practical life experiences and real-world examples. Lastly, you must speak to them clearly when introducing new words to expose them to the right pronunciation (avoid baby talk!).

Now, let's have a look at some great Montessori-encouraged language activities you can practice with your little one:

- Reading - Use books that have colorful illustrations they can look at while you're reading them stories. The Very Hungry Caterpillar books are a great example. Books with big, bright pictures are great for teaching toddlers colors and new vocabulary.

- Language cards - These cards have illustrations you can show your child while introducing new vocabulary or practicing what they already know. At this age, bigger is better. Block books also can serve the same function, although language cards are great for showing your toddler how to make up a story.

- Toy phone - Since kids like to copy adults' behavior so much, this is a really fun and engaging activity you can play with them. Give them a toy phone and pretend you're having a conversation, but let them initiate it first. Toy smartphones with noises and lights really impressed my kids!

Math Activities

All children are exposed to numbers in their day-to-day lives—on calendars, clocks, or other objects of daily use.

However, engaging them in math-related activities can get tricky as you know they can't possibly solve addition or distraction drills. According to the Montessori philosophy, here's what you can do instead:

- Introduce them to the notion of numbers by using magnetic numbers and board. Give them some time to get familiar with them before you try associating each symbol with its name.
- Practice the meaning of 'more' and 'less' by using different objects and dividing them into two piles. Associate each pile with the appropriate 'tag.' You can even use similar objects to help them spot the difference more easily. For example, 'There are more blue cars than red cars.'

Cultural Activities

Introducing your toddler to different cultural activities will help them be exposed to various areas of knowledge they'll encounter as they grow. By exploring various subjects through play, they'll become more interested in learning and exploring different topics. Here are a few Montessori cultural ideas you can tackle:

- Geography - This is best taught using colorful materials and objects, including flat puzzle maps, colored globes, maps of different continents, etc. When presented clearly, they'll help your child understand the different geographical areas in the world. Many Montessori classrooms have group time around a carpet printed with a globe. You can easily find something similar for a home on Amazon.

- Science - In a Montessori environment, toddlers are focused on being introduced to scientific vocabulary. In addition, you can include several things from nature and provide them with knowledge about those objects. At this age, different leaves or fruits and veggies are a great place to start.

- History - You can introduce them to the notion of history by reading different child-appropriate stories about life on earth, historical, and modern times. At the toddler age, these should be kept pretty basic. Again, board books are your best bet here.

- Music - You can successfully teach your little one about music by giving them an idea about dancing and singing. Practice activities that involve these two to keep them engaged and learning.

- Art - This is one of the most important cultural activities to expose your toddler to. It's a great way to teach them about drawing, coloring, and properly holding a pencil.

Chapter 6:
Montessori Principles and Activities for Preschoolers (ages 3-4)

As your little one grows up, you wonder how you can adjust your Montessori environment to better assist their growth. Naturally, you should look into new activities that implement the Montessori principles as your preschooler continually develops and changes needs and preferences. However, keep in mind that no matter how invested you are in the process of searching for new and engaging activities, they still need to align with your child's developmental needs. Ultimately, they should be designed to foster independence and promote real-life skills that will serve your preschooler for years to come.

So, the basics of the Montessori approach stay the same no matter the age group—the types of activities change as children transition from infants to toddlers to preschoolers and further.

Addressing the Developmental Needs and Milestones of Preschoolers in a Montessori Way

First things first, you need to be aware of the developmental needs of your child that arise around this period so that you're able to properly address them. This is the time when you should put more emphasis on self-directed learning experiences, as well as hands-on activities. And although your preschooler will benefit from having more opportunities for learning experiences, you still can't forget to include play activities.

Developmental Needs and Biology

Social development

Although you may not look at your child as a baby anymore, play is still the best option that helps them learn important social skills, such as being cooperative, waiting for their turn, or sharing a toy. During this period, they also learn how to regulate their emotions or express their feelings, and these are just a couple of things that can be practiced with age-appropriate activities. Focusing on your preschooler's social development will help them develop essential skills to form healthy relationships with peers or adults.

Cognitive development

Children often work their cognitive abilities by engaging in different activities that require the use of imagination and problem-solving skills. During this time, they begin to develop their creative and critical thinking, so it's important that you're aware of this and provide a variety of activities to support it. Some good examples you can use are puzzles, blocks, building structures, or engaging in some sensory activities (which you'll discover later).

Physical development

Another aspect you need to focus on is your preschooler's physical development. Although most kids between 3 and 4 are energetic and always running around, you need to introduce them to activities that will help them practice their gross and fine motor skills, coordination, and balance. These will also help them learn more about their bodies, as well as the way they move. So, apart from running, jumping, or dancing, you can also familiarize them with balance beams or climbing structures to further support their development.

Learning

As Dr. Montessori observed, children learn best through exploration and being presented with various hands-on activities. She discovered that play isn't only the most natural but also a very effective way for children to acquire knowledge. This is because they're not only presented with plain information but also having fun discovering on their own. You can encourage them to explore their environment and learn new things about different areas of life through different activities. As a result, preschoolers become more curious and start asking questions in search of answers. This is a great way to set a foundation for future academic learning.

Milestones

To be able to answer your child's developmental needs, you have to be aware of the milestones that should happen around this time. So, for example, they should know by now to say their name and age, answer simple questions, speak more clearly, and tell short stories. Moreover, their vocabulary is between 250 and 500 words, allowing them to engage in simple conversations with peers or adults.

In addition to these, there are several other milestones that happen when they're between 3 and 4 years old.

Cognitive milestones

You'll notice that your child starts asking plenty of questions. Although you might find this annoying at times, it's very important that you don't ignore or disregard them and try to provide age-appropriate answers every time. Here are the cognitive milestones preschoolers reach:

- Differentiate between and correctly name colors
- Understand the notions of 'same' and 'different'
- Remembers stories or events
- Sort objects by different characteristics
- Recognize objects and pictures
- Follow commands
- Count and understand the notion of time
- Successfully completes puzzles appropriate for their age

Movement milestones

Although your child has probably made the biggest movement advancement while they were toddlers, you'll notice that they continue to be on the move even as preschoolers. So, between the ages of 3 and 4, your child should:

- Climb confidently

- Walk forward and backward without being clumsy
- Kick, throw, and catch a ball
- Ride a tricycle or run without stumbling
- Hop and step on one foot
- Climb stairs

Knowing the milestones your kid is expected to achieve will better prepare you for what you should expect and where to focus your support. If you're struggling with evaluating any of the above, bring your concerns to your pediatrician. A physician can help identify any biological causes of developmental delays. As you probably learned by now, the Montessori approach is all about supporting children and allowing them to grow at their own pace by offering gentle guidance only. So, use this knowledge as your guide when looking for engaging ways to promote optimal growth and development of your preschooler.

Respecting Emotions, Setting Limits, and Discipline in the Preschooler's Years

The Montessori approach is built upon the idea of giving children freedom and respecting them for who they are. This is why you need to be very careful and consider all aspects of your child's individuality so they can thrive. Given that the most significant development is achieved when they're little, you must be familiar with all the key things you need to pay attention to, including their emotions and establishing discipline and healthy limits.

Identifying and Acknowledging Their Emotions

It's essential to acknowledge your child's emotions, no matter how overreacting they might seem in certain situations. While creating this unique approach, Dr. Montessori was very clear about the importance of treating children with the utmost respect. And if you spend some time observing and trying to understand their needs, you'll see that the reaction they're presenting is quite justified. Don't approach a situation from your own standpoint. Remember that your preschooler is just a child who hasn't yet fully developed the idea of reasoning in their head. So, the emotional responses you'll come across correspond to their development level. Once you understand that, dealing with it will become so much easier.

Children aged 3-4 aren't still masters of their emotions. Although their age allowed them to tackle this development area, they still haven't completed it. Like every other process, this isn't something that happens by itself. As your preschooler is gradually acquiring their language, critical thinking, and other skills, they'll become more able to identify and control their feelings as they arise. During this stage, children are still becoming acquainted with their emotional expressions, learning what different feelings mean and how to express or control them properly.

So, what can you do to support their emotional development while respecting their emotions? The Montessori approach views this type of development as something that can be achieved through fostering healthy relationships and interactions. Instead of trying to control your child, telling them what they should or shouldn't do, you should offer your help through guidance. This will show that you respect their feelings and doings and help them learn how to control and regulate their emotions.

The most important thing for emotional development is to be able to self-regulate. Once your child learns this, they shouldn't have a problem controlling or appropriately expressing their emotions as they grow up. It's a skill that will serve them for a lifetime.

How to Set Limits for Your Preschooler and Why It is Important

Another very important aspect of creating a Montessori environment that will assist your child as they grow and develop is to set limits. When I say limits, I don't mean that they should be expressed loudly and clearly in a way that your child sees them as prohibitions. Instead, they should be very thoughtfully established to allow your child to thrive around them without disrupting their freedom.

Think about what is important to you as a family that you want your child to learn from the youngest of age. It could be that you're only eating at the dinner table and not on the floor or bed, or perhaps everyone should clean up their mess once they're done doing a particular activity. Use these as guidance points when considering which limits you'd like to set around your preschooler. And if you've already followed the Montessori approach for your child's upbringing, you already have some limits. In this case, think about whether there's something else you need to introduce or perhaps something you think shouldn't be a limit anymore. Adjust the setting to be age-appropriate and let your child thrive!

Something to keep in mind is how you're presenting those limits in front of your kid. Now that they're bigger, they can understand explanations more, so you can use this to your benefit. For example, you can make sure that the limits you set are clear and that they reflect your family or cultural values. In addition, ensure that you're giving good explanations of why a certain rule is set. "You can't hit other kids because you'll hurt them" or "We can't continue playing now because it's time for lunch" are a couple of examples that should give you an idea of how to do the explanation. As I already mentioned, keep adjusting the limits as your child grows so that they're appropriate for their cognitive and emotional stage of development.

A Parenting Guide for Disciplining Your Preschooler

Another important aspect of creating your home Montessori environment is to set the ground for discipline. This doesn't mean you should restrict or punish your preschoolers every time they do something wrong or inappropriate. However, they also shouldn't be allowed to do whatever they like. It's all about building an inner sense of good behavior that would serve them even when they're grown-up adults.

Here are a few ideas you should model your preschooler discipline approach around:

No rewards, punishments, or bribes

All three are examples of extrinsic motivation, and Montessori principles are aimed toward developing an intrinsic one. Your preschooler shouldn't be raised to look upon others to do something—they should be self-motivated to do so. Instead of always comparing them with other kids or their older siblings, do some reasoning to help them understand why they should or shouldn't do something.

Communicate respectfully

Just because they're your children doesn't mean you should look at them as immature. Preschoolers have plenty of time left to grow and develop into adults, but nothing should stop you from being respectful when communicating with them. Your preschool child can now notice whether you value or support them, so shouting or constantly saying 'no' won't help you achieve your discipline goals.

Solve problems together

Children aged 3-4 are now more capable of doing some reasoning, so why not include them in the problem-solving process? Instead of bribing them to do something, try to devise ways to involve them in the process. For example, think about how to motivate them to leave the playground even when they would rather still stay at and play or how to help you set up the table. Try to convey the idea that preschoolers are doing something not because they need to but because it shows that they're caring for the rest of your family members.

Suggestions of Montessori Practical Life Activities, Sensorial Materials, Language Activities, Mathematics Materials, and Cultural Activities for Preschoolers

When it comes to Montessori activities for preschoolers, you'll probably notice that there's not really a drastic difference from those applicable to toddlers. The biggest distinction, however, comes from the fact that they're more advanced—created to answer the needs of preschoolers. As children become more capable of learning during this time, your curriculum should contain more activities that engage their learning capabilities while encouraging play.

Have a look at the examples below to become inspired about incorporating activities that tackle different aspects of their growth and development. You can even use those as a guide when creating your own exercise versions.

Practical Life Activities

Raising your child in a Montessori environment means that you're actively preparing preschoolers for the life that happens after their years of official education come to an end. So, the earlier you introduce some real-life activities into the upbringing process, the easier it will be for them to master and utilize them as they grow up.

One of the greatest benefits of teaching your preschooler practical life activities is not only because you'll get help with your household chores. More importantly, they'll get a sense of what goes into caring for their home, garden, or pet, which will teach them thoughtfulness.

Here are some examples of practical activities based on the Montessori method you can introduce to your preschooler:

- Setting the table
- Wash the windows
- Tying their own shoes
- Match bottles to lids
- Prepare their meals or help in the preparation of those for the whole family
- Taking care of plans
- Washing or wiping dishes
- Caring for your pet

Sensorial Activities

The sensorial development of your preschooler is yet another important aspect of their growth. Now that they're bigger, they can engage in various sensorial activities. These work on developing your child's five senses, teaching how to use them, and learning about the environment.

Try applying these sensorial activities based on the Montessori philosophy with your preschooler:

- **Fabric box** - This is a classic activity from the Montessori curriculum that you can use. Through this, you can get your child to match fabrics with similar textures, which allows them to work on their tactile senses. You can also ask them to describe the materials in their words, whether they're soft, bumpy, etc.

- **Sound box** - Fill several cardboard boxes or cylinders with different items. Your child is then supposed to shake them and explore the variety of sounds they produce. Moreover, you can ask them to match the boxes that produce similar sounds and make sound pairs.

- **Building a tower** - This is yet another classic Montessori curriculum activity. For those of you who aren't familiar with it, it consists of different-sized blocks the child is supposed to build a tower with. Through trial and error, they learn they should start by using the biggest block at the bottom and the smallest one at the top.

Language Activities

Language is yet another important thing to focus on while your child goes through preschool development. These activities are powerful learning tools for children aged 3-4, as they help them gain confidence, improve their vocabulary, and, naturally, their self-expression. This is the time when they'll start to act more independently, and they'll enjoy being involved in different activities.

You can easily use your weekend trips in nature as great language-learning opportunities and engage your child. According to the Montessori method, here's what you can do:

- **Storytelling** - Bedtime stories aside, you can introduce a different type of storytelling activity while spending time in nature. Give your child a bag and instruct them to collect different objects so that they can later create a story, including them.

- **Sequencing** - Undoubtedly one of the best pre-reading activities, sequencing with plants is very easy to do for 3 and 4-year-olds. Try to make them think about different situations using their critical and logical thinking, recognize, and come up with a story. This activity consists of several pictures that tell a story if placed in the right order. Let them use their logic to put the cards in order, and then ask them to talk about the story they tell.

- **Just one thing** - Pick an object from your surroundings and initiate a storytelling activity that revolves around the object. For example, if you choose a tree, you can provoke them to talk about how it was little once and has grown so tall over the years or how it makes a home to different insects or birds. It's a great way to practice their vocabulary and logical thinking in story creation.

Math Activities

Preschoolers are more aware of the notion and appearance of numbers as they come across them on a daily basis. This is the ideal time to introduce them to more engaging math-related activities to help them develop different math concepts. From counting to using measurements as you're cooking, many activities are suitable for a Montessori home environment.

As your child is now older, you can be freer in choosing the learning materials to use as you won't have to worry about choking hazards or items they'll potentially hurt themselves with. The Montessori philosophy suggests sticking to using printable cards as they allow for a great variety of activities. For example, you can use cards to introduce simple activities with addition (1+1, 2+1) or have different numbers printed so the child can put the correct number of objects in front of each card.

Cultural Activities

Regarding the cultural aspect of development, the Montessori method suggests that it's very important that you now actively expose them to different cultural topics. It's easiest to start by learning some geography, although you shouldn't forget to include other activities. For example, you can use cards with Earth's continents, each presented in a different color. This is a great way to help them explore and learn their different sizes and shapes and even connect their appearance to their names. Another one is to use cards with flags of countries (including their own), so they'll learn to recognize different geographical areas by looking at their flags.

These are just a couple of examples of how you can introduce culture into your preschooler's Montessori curriculum. Feel free to discover more age-appropriate activities and introduce them when you feel it's most appropriate and that your child would have the greatest benefit from.

Chapter 7: Montessori Principles and Education for School-Age Children (ages 5-8)

Until now, the majority of activities and practices you introduced to your child to support their development revolved around play. And this was the most appropriate way to assist them as they were galloping through the infant, toddler, and preschool years. However, once they reach age 5, they're ready to go to kindergarten; you need to become more intentional with how you design the Montessori environment at home. This is when the curriculum you create becomes critical to your kid's development.

However, don't be afraid of how this sounds. You can receive assistance in many ways during this stage, and this book aims to cover the most important ones. I'm here to tell you that, during these years, you don't need to use a strictly-designed syllabus that will divide schooling and Montessori time. These two must still be intentionally connected to offer the greatest benefits. Children in the kindergarten stage are still very young, which means that they're probably mainly encouraged by their individual interests. Of course, you'll need to implement a few additional rules to make a thriving Montessori setting, but the basic principles, such as respect and freedom, still apply.

Addressing the Developmental Needs and Milestones of School-Age Children in a Montessori Way

During this phase of growth, children are still incredibly receptive, soaking up the world. If you remember when I talked about the absorbent mind, this is the stage when it hugely applies. Your school-age child's brain will act like a sponge, ready to absorb most of the environment. In addition, they'll be more focused on themselves and have an increased urge to do things independently. This sense of independence will serve them as they grow, especially if you cultivate it mindfully.

In terms of their developmental needs, here's what you need to know:

Developmental Needs and Biology

In their development, children pass through different phases, each of which is characterized by different needs and accomplishments. There's a special sensitivity level that leads them to explore and ingest everything from their surroundings. Children adapt better to life because they are given the freedom to explore and discover these things on their own.

So, during the kindergarten stage of development, you need to provide them with optimal support that will correspond to their needs. Here is something you need to pay attention to during this stage:

- Your child is in a period of immense physical and 'spiritual' construction
- They need to be shown that they're loved and protected
- They're finessing their coordinated movement
- They need to be exposed to purposeful work
- Their potential for intellectual development is gradually increasing
- They've learned how to express and control emotions
- They can slowly be introduced to the notion of abstract learning

- They're using their imagination for different purposes

Awareness of these important developmental aspects is very important when creating a Montessori environment for them for the first time or if you're simply adjusting to the one they're already used to growing in. Their environment must be changing as they pass through different growth phases, so they'll always be properly challenged. Remember—your child can't experience a significant improvement if they're not properly stimulated. This is why you need to be aware of the developmental needs in the kindergarten stage so that you can create the ideal thriving environment for them.

Milestones

Similar to the notion of developmental needs, every stage of your little one's development is characterized by different milestones. This means that there's a time and place for every achievement to happen, and you need to be aware of those when designing your home Montessori setting. Not only because you have to provide them with different engaging activities to support their growth but also because you'll find it easier to understand their actions or emotions when you know what they're sensitive to.

Here are the milestones school-aged children are expected to reach:

Emotional and social changes

This is a time when they should be more aware of their surroundings and emotional state, so they're learning how to blend these two and balance the behavior they're presenting. So, you should expect them to show more independence and willingness to work alone without your support. They'll also start showing interest in their future and, in a way, "planning" for it. This is when you'll hear them say, "When I grow up, I want to be…" In addition, they'll start to make sense of their place in their social environment and the world. They'll be more aware of the relationships they have with their peers or family members, and the need to be liked and accepted will increase.

Thinking and learning

In terms of cognitive milestones in middle childhood, you'll notice that your kid presents an increased development in their mental skills. They've probably acquired new and better ways to describe experiences and express their feelings and thoughts. In addition, the self-focus phase will slowly start to fade out, and they'll start being more considerate of other people in their surroundings. This is also when your child is exposed to two different developmental periods—the Absorbent Mind and the Reasoning Mind. This means they'll slowly outgrow their sensitive stage and become more imaginative and philosophical. Moreover, they start showing more interest in learning practical subjects.

You must show affection and recognize their achievements to support your child through their needs and milestones. In addition, you should assist them in developing their sense of responsibility and showing interest in their kindergarten or school activities. Once they start showing interest in setting goals for their future, you can help set them and ensure they're easily achievable. And despite the fact that you need to practice new approaches, you still shouldn't do the most important ones you've practiced so far, such as reading, fun family activities, and discipline guidance.

Again, if you're struggling with evaluating any of the above, bring your concerns to your pediatrician. Sometimes, a fresh set of eyes helps ease your concerns, or can offer other suggestions to help your child if there are any developmental concerns. Your community, so to speak, should include everyone on the team who is helping you raise your child!

Respecting Emotions, Setting Limits, and Discipline in the School-Age Years

Creating a Montessori environment for your school-aged child to grow in means you have to consider several aspects when designing it. This doesn't only revolve around the physical items it needs to include that will support their growth, such as interactive toys or learning materials. It also means that you must respect their feelings, establish the proper limits, and introduce discipline. I will go over each of these separately so that you'll understand what you're supposed to do.

Their Emotions Matter

Respect is one of the basic things in every healthy parent-child relationship. However, this period is especially vital for their development. Of course, this doesn't exclusively apply on the child's part, but also on yours. When school-age children feel that their parents respect them, they're more likely to grow into adults with more self-respect than those who lack this element while growing up. This means that you have a direct role in the development of their sense of worth, which is vital at this moment and requires that you know how to promote it. Therefore, make sure to apply the following approaches based on the Montessori method to help them thrive:

Listen actively

One of the first things you can do to show your school-aged child you're acknowledging their emotions is actively listening to them. Whenever they're trying to tell you something, make sure you focus your full attention on them, trying to see things from their perspective.

Acknowledge their feelings

You should be considerate of their feelings in addition to paying close attention to what they have to say. Although they might not express their emotions like you do, it doesn't mean their feelings aren't valid. By validating their feelings, you're letting them know you care about them and that their emotions are very important to you.

Show that you trust them

Another thing that's very important, apart from being respectful, is to show that you trust them. Give your school-aged child appropriate responsibilities without interrupting them while they're working on them so they know you have full trust in them.

Respect boundaries

In the same way, you want your boundaries to be respected by others; your child needs that, too. This means you shouldn't intentionally invade their personal space or push them to do things they don't want to do.

Show love

Showing your school-aged child love and care will make them feel valued. This will help them grow into respectful adults who are considerate of others' feelings as well as their own.

Be a role model

By now, you've probably heard many times that children often copy or shape themselves in the image of their parents. So, the best thing you can do is model kindness and respect so they can know which feelings to emphasize as they grow.

A unique and very effective way to set limits for school-age children

Growing up in a Montessori environment means you should give your child the freedom to develop in their own way. However, no level of freedom will be productive for your school-aged child if no boundaries are established—which is the next thing you should focus on.

Setting limits is never easy, but it's crucial if you want to give your child the optimal thriving environment. If you already have some limits set, then make sure to adjust them accordingly so they're appropriate for their age. And if you're just starting out to explore and implement this approach, there are a few things you need to keep in mind:

- Ensure that the environment you create has clear boundaries. Try to find a balance between saying 'yes' and 'no' and keep the middle ground.

- Make sure that their attention is focused on you while you're explaining some rule so that you'll know they've heard what you said.

- When setting your limits, be empathetic toward them so they'll be more receptive.

- Establish only those limitations you feel are necessary to be put in place without making the environment seem too restrictive.

- The earlier you introduce limits to your child's upbringing, the easier it will be for them to become independent and develop their social skills.

However, setting these limits doesn't mean they're there to stay for good. Monitor how your child responds to the environment so you can observe how they respond to it.

Disciplining Your School-Aged Child the Montessori Way

Children aged 5-8 already attend school or kindergarten. So, this can make it a little trickier to establish discipline because they're not growing in their home environment exclusively. Switching between two different surroundings can make it harder to establish certain principles of discipline, especially if your child finds it hard to use those you set at home while they're in school. However, the sensitivity of their age makes it ideal for laying the foundation for the development they'll build on as they grow up.

Here's what it means when I say establishing discipline in the Montessori environment your school-aged child will grow in:

Don't overreact

The odds are your child is going to do something out of line, which will make you tempted to demonstrate a reaction. However, this doesn't mean you should let your emotions overpower your control. Always try to stay calm and nonreactive when approaching the situation, and don't punish them, as this will cause a counter-effect.

Be respectful

As I already mentioned above, it's very important that you're respectful toward your school-aged child. Use clear and concise language when you're setting your boundaries and expectations. The practice has shown that children are more responsive to direct and clear information as they see it as consistent and reliable.

Let them know what you're expecting from them

This is the best way to ensure your child will follow and meet your expectations. For example, if they're expected to do something later in the day, you can give them a heads-up earlier so they'll know what they should do. This also works with their school activities. For example, if you notice that they've returned from school and went to watch TV immediately, you can remind them they're supposed to do their homework first by saying, "What is that thing you need to do once you return home?" or "What's the first rule of the house?"

No bribes, punishments, or rewards

This is another core basis of the Montessori philosophy that applies to all ages. Remember that establishing discipline isn't about bribing or punishing your child when they do something wrong. At the same time, you shouldn't reward them or give excessive praise when they do something right. The core of the Montessori approach is to provide intrinsic, not extrinsic, motivation. This means that children should be willing to do the task independently and not rely on the reward they'll receive if they complete it.

Suggestions of Montessori Practical Life Activities, Sensorial Materials, Language Activities, Mathematics Materials, and Cultural Activities for School-Age Children

In a Montessori environment, the focus should be put on hands-on learning and on giving individualized instructions. When it comes to incorporating activities that will support your school-aged child's growth, it's important to remember that they need to be adapted not only to their age but also to their needs and interests.

Here are a few ideas about different types of activities you can engage your child at home:

Practical Life Activities

As we have already established, the Montessori principle you want to include in the prepared environment for your school-aged child is focused on building real-life life skills they will use in the future. Now that your child is older, you can engage them in various activities that don't always revolve around play. So, for example, the Montessori method implies inviting them to help you with your household chores and letting them fold clothes or towels. In addition, you can show them how to properly water your plants so they can do it together with or instead of you. When cooking, you can ask them to help peel the vegetables you will use, so they'll practice their fine motorics and coordination. Once they become acquainted with the safe use of a knife, you can also ask them to help you cut fruits and vegetables. They can even make their own fruit snacks from time to time!

If you have a habit of involving every family member in the preparation of the meal, you can ask your child to help set the table. This will make them feel like they're making a big contribution by simply being included in this routine.

Sensory Activities

The sensorial activities you will introduce will help the child work on refining their senses. As a result, they'll be able to better understand or engage in new experiences. Now that your children are actively preparing or already going to school, they're able to understand more complex ideas.

- Temperature discrimination: Introduce them to the notion of temperature and let them explore the difference between cold and warmth.

- And since they've already gotten in touch with different textures and materials, it should be easier to identify various textures and match objects made of the same material.

You can also help them develop their smell by giving them candles and asking them what each smells of. Let them help you arrange something by instructing them to group different items by size. In addition, you can also make a fun activity to test their senses by covering their eyes and having them try different foods. They should then guess what they've tried, and you can tell them whether they got it right or if they should guess again.

- Sound recognition: You can get them to guess sounds different instruments make and have them group them according to the instrument family they belong to. This will help develop their hearing perception and appreciation for music.

Language Activities

By now, your child will have a larger vocabulary, which they'll actively use to form sentences, tell stories, and engage in lengthy conversations. However, they'll still be open to learning more words and forming more complex utterances, so it's important that you provide them with proper stimulation.

Based on the Montessori method, you should focus on establishing the fundamentals of language learning before you move on to more complex activities. So far, you've sung and read to them, and now it's time to introduce them to how letters sound. Stay away from language learning toys and encourage face-to-face interactions. Limit screen time and exposure to a second language so you don't confuse and alter their progress.

When introducing new vocabulary, make sure you're speaking the words clearly and have them repeat them several times. Even if you notice they have difficulties with uttering certain sounds, their version of a word should be very close to the original one.

Math Activities

Probably, your school-aged child knows how to count and is already introduced to numbers. They can also recognize different numbers from a sequence. According to the Montessori philosophy, the first thing you need to introduce them to is being well-acquainted with the first decimal and the notions of addition and subtraction, and maybe even multiplication and division. Make sure you first present this concept visually by giving them ten blocks and using them to present everything you do.

Moreover, this is when they'll be introduced to different math rules and work with whole numbers and decimals. They should also be taught to present information using graphs and charts and understand additional concepts, such as equivalency, symmetry, and similarity.

Cultural Activities

I believe this will be the best and most interesting part of applying your Montessori method as a parent, especially starting in this age group. These activities are related to different aspects of our culture, including history, geography, science, art, music, etc. Although this is something kids learn at school, there's nothing wrong with coming up with different activities that will help you support their learning at home.

With your preschool child's knowledge in the fields of language and mathematics, they'll be able to explore different science and cultural topics. If you allow them to research the topics that interest them, you can bet they'll become really involved and eager to learn more. This can include anything from history, art, and geography to literature, music, and commerce.

For example, the Montessori method suggests introducing history through large timelines that will give them a visual representation of important historical periods. Geography will focus on Earth, tell its place in the universe, and introduce the child to all planets in the Solar system. Similarly, science will cover things like Earth's rotation, friction, or gravity, and children will be introduced to simple experiments and scientific reports.

Chapter 8:
Montessori Principles and Education for Tweens (ages 9-12)

As a parent, you've probably noticed that your child's development doesn't go in a constant, upward trend. Instead, it sometimes speeds up and other times slows down, featuring all kinds of changes. You need to know that this is an entirely normal growth process, and it's tied to the different stages your child goes through. So, you can't expect them to always be highly receptive or learn new things at an incredibly fast rate. They need a balance in their development, allowing them to grow healthily and avoid becoming overwhelmed. This inconsistent pattern of growth is something every tween goes through, so you need to learn how to properly support it.

Addressing the Developmental Needs and Milestones of Tweens in a Montessori Way

As your child goes through different developmental stages, their needs and milestones constantly change. So, if during their toddler stage, they were incredibly perceptive of the environment as they developed their sensory abilities, you can't expect that they'll do the same once they enter their tweens. Now that they've already mastered this developmental fragment. They'll be focused on learning and acquiring something new—and don't expect it to be at the same speed rate as they learned something else! Here is what you need to know about their developmental needs and milestones between their 9th and 12th age.

Developmental Needs and Biology

During their tween stage, children abandon sensorial exploration and shift their focus to more abstract learning. They now start to better understand the world and concentrate on the bigger picture. What this means is that their exploration turns inward to reasoning and imagination and forming judgments about different topics and issues they come across daily. This is when they first face the need to use morals and reasoning when reaching conclusions or making decisions. From the little child taught how to tell between right and wrong, they've now grown into students who actively question and consider why's that. As a result, they now feel more inclined to think about different ideas, including justice, fairness, and morality. And since they've spent a few years in formal education, they learned much about relationships with their friends and teachers.

From a physical perspective, although a few major changes will happen during this time (permanent teeth, teeth growth, and hair texture change), they overall see a steadier development compared to when they were younger.

The tween years are a very important transition from childhood to adolescence. This is when they slowly abandon some of their early-age habits and slowly prepare for active development leading to adulthood. This is why you need to know how to alter the Montessori environment to support and assist healthy growth.

This can be the first time they face some challenges in school, so it's important that you notice this if they do. Now that they can communicate better, you can openly talk about possible issues and offer assistance. It's important to remember that, no matter at which stage of development they're at, you should never stop acting as a guide and supporting them. Try to put yourself in the role of a friend and enjoy hanging out together. However, don't insist on your involvement in activities—it's always best to let them invite you than to be pushy about doing things together. This can be a very confusing stage for them because they're slowly paving their way toward independence, so they won't want your presence at all times.

Another thing that will change around this period is that they'll probably want to spend more time with their friends. Although this is a natural occurrence, I understand that you might be upset about their safety or this sudden shift from spending all the time with you to slowly beginning to search for a new interactive environment. However, you shouldn't act overly defensive—after all, you know how it is as you've been there before. That is why you need to try to gain their trust so they'll tell you where and with whom they're going to spend their time. This is a very important step to take that they'll practice even when they enter their adolescent years.

Milestones

Similar to the differences they'll experience in terms of their developmental needs, your pre-teenager will also have different milestones to achieve. Between the ages 9-12, your child will be old enough to seek independence, although not mature enough to make every decision for themselves. The end of this stage also marks the beginning of puberty, so their hormones will be all over the place. To properly support their development during these times, it's essential that you know which milestones they are to reach. Here's what to expect:

- They're able to recognize problematic situations and work to reach solutions.
- They use the power of observation to draw conclusions.
- They're learning how to generalize and reach different conclusions.
- Tweens show an increased interest in factual information.
- They're enjoying group school projects in which they can share and hear others' ideas.
- They're more likely to start doing things and projects on their own.
- Learn how to apply factual knowledge to daily life, including different math concepts.
- They're actively interested in trying different hobbies and are eager to spend their free time doing them.

- Experience an increase in their memory capacity and thinking.
- Begin to understand the value of money.
- Become more abstract in their thinking.
- Search for more independence.

Regarding the last point, I must say that you shouldn't let this seeming craving for distance fool you. Even though they'll often show you that they want to spend time on their own or with their friends, this is a very important developmental stage you need to be actively involved. In fact, this is the time when children need their parents most. During all the social changes and challenges, they'll probably face many situations they won't really know how to act upon. Therefore, it's crucial that you observe and offer your guidance and understanding and find ways to support them during these dynamic times.

Respecting Emotions, Setting Limits, and Discipline in Tweens

Following the Montessori approach when raising your child during their pre-teenager period means that you still have to show understanding in their emotions and actions, now perhaps more than ever before. As this is a time of rapid emotional and intellectual growth, your child will really benefit if you show them understanding and compassion. And although they'll feel an increasing need to be independent, it doesn't mean that you should let tweens grow in a setting with no limits and discipline.

Here are some guidelines you can follow to address these aspects:

Tween's Emotions – How to Respect Them

The tween is a developmental stage that serves as a transitional phase between childhood and adolescence. Naturally, your child's body is starting to prepare for the teenage years, which means there's a surge of hormones that might confuse their emotions. And no matter how puzzling this may seem, as a Montessori parent, you need to find a way to properly address them and offer understanding.

Tweens become more aware of their placement in this world, making them question their purpose and role in it. So, your primary goal should be to create a balance between their formal education and personal growth and assist them while they're trying to figure out these answers on their own.

Another important thing that happens during this stage is that they're now more susceptible to peer influence, which isn't always positive. This is when you need to be more aware of their behavior and look for any signs of peer pressure or bullying. If you notice that they've suddenly become more introverted, or if they're starting to display destructive behavior, try to initiate a conversation and find out whether there is something that is bothering them. Don't forget to consider their school as a factor, because they may struggle with a subject.

Generally speaking, tweens become more aware of their identity and actions, and their focus on the inward might make them feel confused or overwhelmed. If you've established a good relationship, you shouldn't find it hard to initiate a conversation or have them talk about their feelings and emotions. At the beginning of this stage, you should try to prepare them for what they can expect over time. Don't desensitize them, but rather remind them that you're always here to be their friend and good listener, and don't force your opinions if they don't ask for one. Be a stable force in their life they can rely on and show respect when they're communicating their emotions either verbally or physically.

What Limits You Set With Your Tween Now Will Set the Tone for the Rest of Their Development

Their need for more freedom and independence doesn't mean you need to eliminate all the limits you've set so far. Even if this is the first time you're interested in creating a Montessori setting for them, you need to set the basis by establishing some ground rules. The tricky part is that you have to do this by not letting your tween feel like they lack freedom. But how do you achieve this?

Growing up the Montessori way or not, your house must've had certain rules everyone needed to follow—your now-tween included. But given the fact that they're longing for more individuality now, you need to think about ways to allow them to pursue their freedom without letting them do whatever they want. So, the first thing you should do is to re-establish a good connection. Tweens seem more distant during his time compared to when they were little kids, but you need to know that good communication is key. Try to set certain expectations and let them see the reasoning behind them, and this will make it easier for them to follow these. If they find it hard to see your point from the first try, try to find a way to explain so they'll understand, making the issue relatable to them. If you notice that they're trying to work their way around the limits, make sure to remind them about your expectations and ask for their cooperation.

Again, good communication is very important during this stage—always, and I mean always—try to reinforce it.

Disciplining Your Tween

Discipline is yet another important thing when designing a Montessori environment for your tween kid. If you've raised your child following those principles so far, the odds are that they've already developed an inner sense of motivation and understanding about which things they should and shouldn't do. But even if you didn't manage to do so by now, know that it's not too late!

If you read the previous chapters, you already know the general Montessori views on this subject, but if you jumped to this period, let me clarify once again. According to the Montessori philosophy, discipline is a form of instruction rather than restriction and punishment. Therefore, your work should be focused on establishing positive discipline and finding a way to help your tween build intrinsic motivation. This means you shouldn't try to motivate them to do something by rewarding them. This isn't a practical way to approach this situation at all because you're only making your tween do something when they know they'll receive a reward afterward. Instead, you should try to get them to see the inner satisfaction they'll get after completing this task, whether physical or emotional.

Another thing you shouldn't do is compare your tween with their siblings or peers. This will only lead to building negative emotions or make them more introverted. Another useful way to establish discipline is to be a model for the child. So, don't just tell them to do something if you don't do the same. Children learn best through actions rather than words, so it's best to set a good example they'll follow. In addition, help them understand the consequences of their actions and allow them to take responsibility. Sometimes, this is the key thing that will help them realize the effect of their actions and refrain from causing harm.

Suggestions of Montessori Practical Life Activities, Sensorial Materials, Language Activities, Mathematics Materials, and Cultural Activities for Tweens

Having a child in their tween years (9-12) means they're already attending formal education for some time. They'll already be introduced to various subjects and activities that are suitable for their age and support their intellectual growth.

However, this doesn't mean you shouldn't engage them in activities at home. After all, the Montessori approach is about promoting life skills, apart from the ones related to education, so it's important that you don't ignore this fact.

Here are some suggestions for various activities you can engage your child in outside their classroom:

Practical Life Activities

Practical life tasks will promote certain responsibilities and prepare your child for the duties they'll encounter once they become adults. These often include household or gardening chores, as this is a great way to actively include your tween in the maintenance of your home and teach them important skills they'll use in the future.

If I had to guess, I would say that they're already engaged in certain daily activities, such as setting the table, helping in preparing meals, or cleaning up after themselves. So, you need to think about new activities that will not only keep them engaged but which they'll also find interesting. Here are a few Montessori method-based suggestions to think about:

- **Repairs** - You can teach this age group to do simple fixing and repairings, such as sewing up a button or doing other small clothing repairs.

- **(New) chores** - Teach them how to organize their wardrobes and change between winter and summer clothes.
- **Meal planning** - You can include them in the decision-making process and even initiate that they try some simple cooking independently. Involve tweens in meal planning, grocery shopping, and cooking. Teach them about nutrition, healthy food choices, meal preparation, and basic kitchen skills. They can explore recipes, learn to follow instructions, and develop an understanding of balanced diets. This will not only provide experience in meal planning but will also make them feel they're responsible for making important decisions.
- **Gardening** - If you have a garden or simply love planting and caring for potted plants inside your home, this is a great activity to include your tween kid in. You can teach them how to plant, water, and care for different kinds of flowers or green plants, and they'll maybe show interest in helping you regularly. Teach them about plant life cycles, soil composition, and the importance of environmental stewardship. Learn together about how to plant and care for

flowers, vegetables, or herbs, learning about sustainable gardening practices.

- **Mindful Movement and Yoga** - Introduce tweens to mindful movement practices such as yoga, tai chi, or mindfulness-based exercises. These activities promote body awareness, stress reduction, and overall well-being. Encourage them to try different in-person classes or online videos so they can really start to get a feel for what works for them individually.
- **Geocaching and Treasure Hunts** - Organize geocaching or treasure hunt activities for tweens, allowing them to use GPS devices or maps to search for hidden treasures. This activity promotes problem-solving, navigation skills, and outdoor exploration. There are many geocaching clubs online; search for a local, kid-friendly option.

Sensory Activities

Often, children who started going to school, especially after they entered their tween years, slowly begin to be left out of the sensorial activities they used to practice when they were little. It's true, they shouldn't be exposed to the same activities constantly, since they're continually growing and their needs change. However, it doesn't mean that they should be left entirely out.

- **Science experiments:** Let's look into some of the activities according to the Montessori method that you can practice with your tween: making DIY glow-in-the-dark sand, experimenting with making glowing ice and salt, practicing hearing sounds with different pitches, or exploring different types of rocks and minerals and learn their names.

- **Nature hikes:** You can also go on a family trip in nature and have them try to guess different sounds. It's a fun activity your whole family can engage in! Organizing outdoor excursions like nature hikes, camping trips, or orienteering activities also promotes practical life skills. These experiences allow tweens to connect with nature, develop outdoor survival skills, and foster a sense of environmental appreciation.

Language Activities

Now that they're pretty knowledgeable about the language they're speaking (conversational and written), you might wonder how you can engage them in some language activities that will still be interesting to them.

- **Family book club:** The Montessori philosophy encourages joining a book club if they're interested in reading, practicing creative writing, or enrolling in a competition. This might be an option at your local library, and if not, you could start a family book club in which each family member gets to take turns choosing the book.

- **At-home debates:** This is also the time they can start actively participating in debates, so you can initiate a conversation about a topic they're interested in, as this is a great language exercise.

- **Drama clubs or at-home theatre play:** While also a cultural activity, encouraging tweens to express themselves through drama and theatrical performances also builds language skills. They can participate in improvisation exercises, create short skits, or even collaborate on full-scale productions, promoting creativity and teamwork.

Math Activities

Children aged 9-12 will already be familiar with every basic math principle of operation, as they'll learn and practice this at school. And if you're wondering how you can engage them and promote this sphere of development at home, you can achieve that in several ways.

- **Memorization games:** The Montessori method encourages you to consider appropriate memorization games for their age. You can also use multiplication, division, or fraction boards to let them exercise at home. Plus, this is a great time to introduce them to algebra, so you can research activities that include solving equations or exploring patterns.
- **Coding and Computer Programming:** Introduce tweens to coding and computer programming through age-appropriate coding languages or visual programming tools. They can learn the basics of coding, problem-solving, and computational thinking and even create simple interactive programs or games.

- **DIY Projects and Woodworking:** If you or someone in your community has the necessary skills, teach tweens basic woodworking skills, allowing them to create their own small projects. They can learn to use hand tools safely, measure and cut wood, and construct simple structures like birdhouses or shelves.

Cultural Activities

Culture is yet another important aspect children should explore during their tween age. You might be surprised by how excited they can be about indulging in these types of activities. They'll now be able to use these games to learn and link different cultural aspects together. For example, they'll be able to look at Earth from a geographical and social perspective. You can tackle science by engaging in experiments that can be safely done in a home environment, like those listed in the sensory activity section. This also promotes the hands-on approach Montessori is focused on, which will keep your child engaged and increase their learning.

- **Science museum field trips:** You can also involve your tween in organizing educational field trips to science centers, nature reserves, or local research institutions. These trips provide tweens with hands-on experiences, exposure to scientific concepts, and the opportunity to interact with experts in various scientific fields.

- **Explore ethnic cuisines:** Who says that going out for your Sunday launch can't be an insightful activity? You can go to a place serving a different cuisine and let your child taste something they haven't tried before. You can even inspire them to research what a certain meal means to the country and to the people it comes from. Tweens can research traditional recipes, learn about cultural practices related to food, and even help prepare dishes from around the world.
- **Art projects and music:** When it comes to art, music, or physical activities, this is something they're already introduced to in their formal education. Make sure that you're familiar with what they do at school to make a connection to the related activities you do at home. For example, if they're working on creative mosaics, you can buy suitable materials so they can engage in a similar activity at home. This can reinforce and expand their skills and sensitivities and can work on their imagination. In terms of music, you

can introduce them to the notion of folk songs, historical ballads, and anthems. This great activity will help them learn more about their own or some other country's history and music.

- **Community Research Projects:** Encourage tweens to engage in research projects focused on their local community. They can investigate historical landmarks, interview community members, or document cultural traditions, contributing to their understanding of local history and social dynamics.
- **Film Analysis and Storytelling:** Introduce tweens to the art of filmmaking and storytelling. They can analyze movies or short films, learn about narrative structures, and even create their own films or multimedia presentations to convey their ideas or tell stories.

Overall, you should feel free to search for different activities to engage your child in while ensuring they correspond to their age and developmental stage. At the same time, these should correspond to the basic Montessori principles you're already familiar with, ensuring the best thriving environment for your child during all stages of their growth. Remember, the Montessori approach encourages students to follow their interests and take ownership of their learning. These activities for tweens should align with that principle, allowing them to explore their passions, develop independence, and engage in hands-on experiences. Montessori activities for tweens foster their holistic development and cultivate a lifelong love of learning by providing a supportive and engaging environment.

Chapter 9:
Montessori Principles and Education for Teenagers (ages 13-17)

The Montessori approach is all about supporting children during their different stages of development by applying its principles. It concentrates on providing the optimal thriving environment and giving them freedom and individuality. And despite the claim of many that this is an approach suitable for preschool children and those attending early elementary, that's not true. In fact, Montessori principles can be adjusted to apply to children of all ages, from infants to teens. The key to successfully implementing these is to adapt the knowledge and practices to properly support teen's growth.

To continue practicing the Montessori approach as a parenting method for the first time, here is everything you need to know to make your venture successful.

Addressing the Developmental Needs and Milestones of Teenagers in a Montessori Way

As they grow, children face various challenges and show different developmental needs. Every stage is different in a specific way, and it's up to you to be familiar with the needs and milestones they're expected to go through so that you can better understand their behavior. To succeed in creating a thriving Montessori environment for them, you need to be aware of these and know how to address them.

Have a look at the developmental needs and milestones that characterize children's teenage period:

Developmental Needs

The beginning of this period marks the child entering into puberty. This means there will be many changes in their emotions and moods. Many psychologists who have closely monitored every phase of kids' development have noted that this period resembles the one they experienced from birth to age six, not in terms of how children are physically developing but regarding the extent of the transformation teenagers are going through. Their characters once again shift to being unstable, and they begin to show signs of rebellion and indiscipline. This is also when they're actively preparing to enter adulthood, which is why it's important that you also focus on their education. Given that, after the teenage period is over, your child will become a member of society, it's very important that you implement a holistic approach to meeting their needs.

You might notice that your child sometimes struggles with expressing emotions and managing frequent mood swings. This is why you must give your best and stay calm when communicating with them, as overreacting will also worsen the situation. Try to understand that their current behavior is simply a part of their natural development pace, so be understanding and respectful toward them.

Apart from these psychological challenges, your teenager will also experience a major change in their physical appearance. Be wary of how these make them feel, as not all of them are prepared to welcome these transitions open-handed. This is when it's very important to maintain quality communication so they'll feel that their home is their safe space—somewhere where they can speak about their concerns and find understanding and support.

The main reason children find it hard to vocalize their feelings is that they're new to them, so they still haven't figured out a way to express them.

In addition to this, they are also supposed to prepare for what awaits them after finishing secondary and high school. So, you will have to find a way to show you understand them and provide guidance through this period without neglecting their need for independence and freedom. After all, they're now slowly progressing to their grown-up stage and need to be prepared for the responsibilities that await.

Milestones

Just like your child is facing different developmental needs you need to address, they're also expected to reach different milestones. In the process of actively shifting from their middle childhood to the teenage period, many drastic changes happen on both physical and mental/emotional levels. As I said, in terms of the extent of transformation that's going on during this time, psychologists like to compare the teenage phase with the first phase of a child's development. This is because of all the drastic changes during this period, changing children's physical and mental state as they slowly begin to become a grown-up.

Here are the most notable milestones that you should expect your teenager to reach by the time they finish this phase:

- Teenagers become more capable of abstract thinking

- They show more interest in philosophy, politics, or other socially-related issues
- They begin to think long-term, considering their future
- Children become more aware of the consequences of their actions, especially on an academic level
- They set goals and devise plans on how they can achieve them
- They start to consider their social standing, so you'll often find them comparing to their friends or peers
- They're more susceptible to peer influence and worry about being accepted by others
- Teenagers are more actively looking for independence
- They start to become interested and involved in romantic relationships
- Their bodies change drastically, and they slowly start to look more like adults than children
- Teenagers indulge in deeper moral thinking, especially at the beginning of this stage

- Their intellectual interests expand and become more valuable
- Lastly, they seldom think about the meaning of life and how they'll make a better place for themselves in the world

As you can see, your teenager is expected to accomplish a lot of things. From dealing with all the sudden physical changes to thinking about their future and actively participating in building it (on an academic level), there is quite some work they're expected to get done. However, your understanding, guidance, and selfless support are very important to help them move through this phase more easily. Make sure you're selfless in considering their emotions and needs during this time so they don't lose the sense of growing up in a supportive and understanding environment.

Respecting Emotions, Setting Limits, and Discipline in the Teenage Years

Once you become familiar with the developmental needs and milestones your teenage child is expected to have, you must know how to properly address them. After all, understanding all of this is useless if you don't know how to apply it to the

Montessori environment you want to establish as well as to yourself.

As with creating a setting that closely follows the Montessori teaching and principles for any other age group, designing one for your teenager should, more or less, include the same elements. This means that you need to show respect toward their emotions and provide them with the freedom they're yearning for, but still implement important limits and discipline.

The Most Important Period to Respect Their Emotions

If you don't have an older kid who has already gone through their teenage period, you've probably heard a lot about how this period affects children. And the majority of other people's 'insights' were negative. I'm talking about eye-rolling, ignoring, talking back, unwillingness to listen to your intentional advice, etc. However, not every teen acts the same during these years, and their growing environment greatly impacts their behavior. The goal of applying the Montessori principles in creating a thriving setting for your teenager is to give them a healthy and thriving surrounding where they'll grow and develop. And given the pre-determined biological changes they're expected to embark on, you must learn how to respond properly.

When it comes to teenagers' emotions, it's safe to say that they'll undergo a rollercoaster. You might notice that they're testing your patience and challenging your authority, giving negative comments and being more irritable than they used to be. These hormonal outbursts will confuse them, and they'll often react a certain way, not because they're determined to hurt or provoke you but because they won't know a better way to express their feelings. Therefore, you must understand their emotions and be supportive to achieve a positive impact.

The Montessori approach considers emotions an essential part of each child's development. Given this information, neglecting or staying ignorant of them is completely inappropriate. Instead, as a parent, you should focus on creating a safe environment where your child can express their feelings without fearing being judged or ignored. Whenever they're having an emotional outburst, act in a way that will help them calm down before you engage in a conversation. Let them know that you're willing to understand and support them—not just to get over with yet another outburst. Try not to show any sign of criticism and validate their emotions. When your teenager knows their home is a safe space, they'll be willing to communicate their emotions and concerns, knowing that you'll understand and support them.

Setting Limits Doesn't Have to be a Mission Impossible With Your Teen

If it's your first time giving the Montessori method a thought, then you should first know that there's a large emphasis on freedom. But this doesn't mean that you should let your child do whatever they want—on the contrary, you should create an environment with certain limits that will allow your teen to move freely within them. I know this might sound very hard to achieve at the beginning, but in reality, it's not. You have to think about which rules and limitations are important for you and your whole family and establish those around your home.

The need for limits and boundaries comes from creating a safe and responsible environment for your teen. So, they should enjoy the freedom to speak and be heard and the freedom to explore, experiment, and create according to their thinking. At the same time, they should also be able to choose what they want and don't want to do, so you shouldn't force them to do something they're not interested in. However, if this concerns a certain rule that all your family abides by, then a simple conversation and reasoning should do the trick.

Please be clear when setting your expectations and explain the consequences of such. I'm not talking about punishment, but something that is likely to happen if they don't respect someone else. Speaking of respect, you should always rely on the power of respectful and productive communication, as this is the best way for teens to see the reasoning behind their actions.

Another thing you can do is involve them in the rule-setting process so that you can establish a respectful relationship when both of you will respect each other's boundaries.

How to Discipline Your Teen – Yes, It Is Possible!

When it comes to the Montessori philosophy and your teen, you should inspire an intrinsic motivation to do things without threatening, punishing, or comparing them to other peers, siblings, or adults. It's simply a way to positively assist as your teen grows and not reward or punish them depending on their actions. However, considering that the teenage years are the period when your child will probably present some undesirable, even negative behavior, you might wonder how you can design your home setting to follow Montessori principles. Although you may find it harder initially, this venture is achievable.

Clearly setting your expectations and ground rules is the first step to establishing discipline. Consider certain rules that apply to everyone and explain why following them is important to your teenager. If, for example, you're all sitting at the dinner table at 7 p.m., explain to them why it's essential to do the same. You may observe some rebellion at first, and it's crucial that you don't respond with anger and upset. Tell them that it's imperative for you to keep this kind of 'tradition' and that their presence means a lot. Despite being in a period of emotional turmoil, your teenager is a grown child who will be able to see the reasoning behind your words. Use understanding and encouraging language to make it easier for them to comply with rules.

In those moments leading to conflict, actively include them in resolving the issue instead of just giving solutions. Sometimes, you'll also have to reach a compromise, but both sides must actively participate in solving a particular problem.

Suggestions of Montessori Practical Life Activities, Sensorial Materials, Language Activities, Mathematics Materials, and Cultural Activities for Teenagers

Your teenage child is now confidently pacing through their middle and high school years and is probably engaged in various activities. This often doesn't involve school activities only, but also some they're attending outside of their formal education's curriculum. Maybe they're practicing some sports, broadening their knowledge in a foreign language, or dedicating some time to practicing a hobby they're interested in. However, this doesn't mean that you can't think about other engaging activities they can practice alone or with your whole family.

And before I continue to deal with this topic, I must mention that you shouldn't make your teen do anything they're not interested in. The Montessori approach clearly advocates freedom in which children should explore their own passions and interests and actively participate in them. So, you should feel free to introduce any of the following to your teenage child, but keep in mind that they might not be interested in doing all of those. Ideally, you'd already know which field they're more curious to explore, and you'll suggest related activities.

Here are a few areas you can consider:

Practical Life Activities

As you probably know, the Montessori approach promotes a healthy way of raising and nurturing children so they'll grow into complete, independent, and responsible adults. Due to the nature of this approach, teens aren't only supposed to focus on their formal education. Still, they should also practice certain activities that are applicable in real life.

Some of these change over time as your child is growing up, just like their needs shift. Another reason why these vary is that you need to provide your teen with a diverse setting in which they won't get bored. Although establishing a certain routine can be very beneficial, repeating the same activities over the years might not have such a positive effect.

So, here are a few suggestions for real-life Montessori method-based activities you can indulge your teenager in:

- **(New) chores** - Helping around the home is something that all kids should do, no matter their age. However, their tasks and responsibilities will change as they grow and develop. For example, if they weren't supposed to use a knife when preparing meals or use yard equipment, they can now probably do both. Introducing new opportunities for teens to help around the house as a family project can include yard work, laundry, or walking and washing pets. Connect chores to interests, like for those interested in science, how laundry can eliminate mold and other pathogens from our clothes, or for environmentalists, how yard work helps to prepare the earth for a fruitful spring, etc.

- **Meal prep and cooking** - When it comes to meal preparation, allowing teens to take over more of the process will help them acquire a very important life skill (cooking) and feel like they contribute a lot to the household. You can teach them a few easy and healthy recipes they can make even on their own.
- **(New) Repairs** - You can also show them how to do higher-level home repairs. Depending on your child's age, you can teach them how to do basic plumbing, change a bike tire, or replace a lightbulb. This is a great way to inspire them to be more self-sufficient when they grow up.

- **Time management skills** - These are very important for every individual, so they should learn them as early as possible. You can introduce these by instructing them to come up with their own study or activity plan so they'll learn how to effectively manage their time and follow their schedule.
- **Leadership Development** - Offer opportunities for teenagers to develop leadership skills through activities such as encouraging leading group projects, organizing events, or taking on leadership roles in school clubs or organizations. This can be achieved at home by putting your child in charge of a weekend outing or even a weekend trip.
- **Mindfulness and Yoga** - This is mentioned in the tween chapter already, but I'm including it here again because it is such an important skill for emotional regulation. Introduce or reintroduce teenagers to mindfulness practices and yoga to promote self-awareness, stress management, and overall well-being. Offer guided meditation sessions or yoga classes tailored to their age group.

Sensory Activities

When it comes to practicing sensory activities in accordance with the Montessori philosophy, they don't differ very much from those you used to practice in the previous development stage. So, in order to support their sensorial development, here are a few activity suggestions you can use:

- **Mosaic making** - Now that teens have more developed senses, they can easily notice similar shades and differentiate between them. They'll also have a trained eye for textures, so this activity that involves matching hues and textures can be a great way to practice their vision, develop art appreciation, and practice creative recycling of everyday materials!
- **Musical artist exploration** - The teen years are when many of us develop our tastes for different musical genres. Encourage your teen to try and find one artist or song from as many genres as possible. Ask them why they like other genres more than others or how each genre makes them feel.
- **Arts and Crafts** - While this is obviously an activity for any age, teens can encourage and foster creativity and self-expression through artistic activities such as painting, sculpting, pottery, or other crafts.

Encourage teenagers to explore different art forms and express their emotions and ideas through visual arts.

Language Activities

To practice all aspects of the language they've learned so far, you can do plenty of activities as a whole family, not just individual ones that will affect your teenager. For example, the Montessori method encourages you to initiate a debate on a topic you know they're interested in and get them to express their viewpoints in a healthy way without trying to convince others by imposing their opinion. In addition, you can practice some complex vocabulary-building exercises, teach them how to do in-depth research on a certain topic, and many more. These language activities will be very helpful as they grow up and start college, or even after they begin their work career.

Some concrete activity ideas include:

- **Creative Writing and Journalism:** Encourage teenagers to explore their creativity through writing. They can engage in creative writing exercises, write articles for school publications, or even start their own blogs to express their thoughts and interests.

- **Foreign Language Immersion:** Provide opportunities for teenagers to immerse themselves in studying foreign languages. Offer language learning materials, organize language exchanges with native speakers, or even plan trips to countries where the language is spoken.

- **Media Literacy:** Teach teenagers to critically analyze and understand the media they consume. Engage them in discussions about media messages, biases, and the impact of media on society. Encourage them to create media content, such as podcasts or videos, to express their viewpoints.

Math Activities

Teenage years are great for incorporating activities that help apply math ideas to everyday life. These can include:

- **Personal Finance Management:** Introduce teenagers to the world of personal finance by creating activities that teach them about budgeting, saving, investing, and understanding financial concepts such as interest rates, credit scores, and managing expenses.

- **Entrepreneurship Projects:** Encourage teenagers to explore their creativity and problem-solving skills through entrepreneurial projects. They can develop business ideas, create prototypes, conduct market research, and learn about marketing, sales, and finance.
- **Critical Thinking and Problem Solving:** Engage teenagers in activities that challenge their critical thinking abilities and problem-solving skills. This can include puzzles, riddles, logic games, and real-world problem-solving scenarios.

Other activities can include recognizing complex geometric shapes in nature or learning about some physics laws that apply to daily life.

Cultural Activities

This is an especially fun age for cultural activities as teens are starting to form individual opinions and identities. Ways to help them connect that individual sense of self to the greater community include:

- **Community Service:** Engage teenagers in meaningful community service activities that allow them to make a positive impact. They can volunteer at local organizations, participate in environmental initiatives, or organize fundraisers for causes they are passionate about.

- **Public Speaking and Debating:** Provide opportunities for teenagers to improve their communication skills by engaging in public speaking exercises and participating in debates. This activity helps them develop confidence, critical thinking, and the ability to express their opinions effectively.
- **Cultural Studies and Comparative Religion:** Help teenagers continue to develop a global perspective by studying different cultures, religions, and belief systems. They can explore traditions, customs, and practices from various parts of the world, fostering tolerance and understanding. This can be achieved through many different activities, like outings to museums, finding educational films, traveling, visiting different restaurants, or even different local religious services.
- **Environmental Awareness and Sustainability:** Educate teenagers about environmental issues and encourage them to take action by engaging in sustainability projects. They can participate in

recycling programs, organize awareness campaigns, or implement eco-friendly initiatives in their community.

Chapter 10:
Montessori-Inspired Learning in College-Age Students (ages 18-21)

As you already learned, Montessori is a unique approach to educating children and assisting them as they grow into complete, independent adults. You know that its principles can be applied as early as during the infant period of a child, but have you ever wondered when is the latest they can be used?

The practice has shown that the Montessori philosophy is holistic and considers several aspects of a child's individuality to design an environment that would provide optimal learning and thriving conditions. So, apart from allowing you to apply its principles during your child's active physical and cognitive development, these can also be useful after they turn 18 and start attending college.

That being said, here is what you and your college-age student should know about implementing the Montessori philosophy.

Addressing the Developmental Needs and Milestones of College-Age Students in a Montessori Way

The period of your child's college years (18-21) is when you'll see how their growth and development are gradually slowing down until it completely stops. So, from a child who has experienced so many growing needs and reaching milestones during each of the previous stages, you'll now look at an almost fully-formed individual ready to undertake the life and academic challenges yet to come. Now, you'll notice that your college-age child can express more critically-based opinions, think and talk about different societal and moral matters, and is almost fully independent in terms of real-life skills they've acquired.

However, I can't say that their process of developing as an individual is completely over. There are still some things they're yet to tackle or refine, which happen during these years when they're supposed to attend college. Here are the most notable events that will likely happen during this time, marking the last stage of your child's development and their official entering into adulthood.

There's a need for self-directed learning

The Montessori approach is about providing optimal learning and development opportunities at the child's own pace. And this is equally important during their earliest and latest years of development. The founder of this approach, Dr. Montessori, stated that children show greater results when given freedom of choice. This means they should be able to show their interest in different subjects or topics and be properly guided to explore and master them.

And since your college child isn't so little anymore, they'll be more capable of performing this self-directed learning. The college environment is the ideal place to practice this because it gives students more freedom in choosing the subjects they want to study and not touch upon those that don't fit their interests. So, how does the Montessori approach align with this? By encouraging children to choose the study courses they favor, be more self-aware about their interests and academic needs, and keep them motivated while they're doing what they ultimately love. Therefore, college students should be able to identify their learning needs, devise their goals, identify the resources that will help them achieve those goals, and ultimately evaluate whether their learning strategies are giving them optimal results.

There's also an increased need for community involvement

As they grow up, children are slowly becoming more and more aware of their place in the community and their contribution to it. It's no wonder that as they reach the last stage of growth, they feel this increasing need to be more involved in society—especially in their college environment.

The Montessori approach puts great value into community involvement, which is why, through its principles, it encourages children to learn more about themselves so they'll know how they can contribute to the community. Children who have grown following this approach will be more self-aware (both of their strengths and weaknesses). As a result, they'll be more confident in their abilities and know how to use them to secure their place in the college community and achieve their goals. And once they do, they'll know they have to value the diversity that's created thanks to the variety of students present there, and they'll know how to take advantage of and use it as a great learning environment.

The need to further learn and explore

Since Montessori education is all about embracing students' individuality and learning according to their interests, it's no wonder that students are often tempted to challenge those and try new things from time to time. And there's no better environment for this than the diverse college one. Here, students come across various opportunities they can choose whether they'd take or not. Often, they feel the need to try something they haven't tried before, so they'll see whether they should dedicate their time to developing a new skill. Apart from school subjects, students also get this opportunity from internships, programs for studying abroad, student exchange possibilities, and more.

Develop critical thinking

Due to the nature of the college environment, especially if the child has grown according to the Montessori principles, they'll now receive the perfect opportunity to further develop their ability for critical thinking. They can do this by actively asking questions, discussing matters that feel important to them during class, and analyzing the information they're presented with.

Another way Montessori supports the development of students' critical thinking is by teaching them they should be interested in detailed research. The college environment also provides them with various opportunities to practice this by providing them with opportunities to engage in various research projects, seminars, and project initiatives.

Forming leadership skills

The goal of the Montessori approach to developing children's individuality and critical thinking often inspires the development of leadership skills. This is a very important aspect of every complete individual. Intertwining this with the college environment, students get more opportunities to work with others, practice their communication skills, and work as a team.

Explanation of How Montessori Principles Can Be Applied to College Education

As I mentioned a few times, the college environment provides the optimal setting for applying Montessori principles. Since Montessori is all about giving complete freedom to students to choose what they're going to learn depending on their interests, you see why the college environment is a good place to practice this.

In this section, I'm going to discuss why it's so important to incorporate the notion of self-centered learning during college. In addition, I'll also give you suggestions about how you can take advantage of the Montessori strategies and incorporate them to enhance your college experience. Give these good considerations to be able to decide which will allow you to experience the greatest learning benefit while you're confidently thriving through your college years.

Discussion of the Importance of Student-Centered Learning in College

The notion of student-centered learning is very important from the Montessorian aspect. This is a very useful way of prioritizing the students' needs and working toward designing a learning strategy that will support their own interests instead of just following an already prepared curriculum. Why is college one of the best environments to practice this type of learning? Because it naturally gives students more freedom to choose what they will learn. This is primarily done when students are allowed to choose between their minor and major. Majors represent the primary fields of study, while minors help them orient toward a more specific area. In fact, these don't even have to be related, so if students struggle to devote themselves to a single area of study, they can choose two.

Students who have grown up following the Montessori approach know more about themselves and their points of interest. Therefore, they can easily translate this into their college environment by choosing subjects that align with their interests. However, this isn't the only reason self-centered learning is important to be practiced in college:

Increasing the ability to solve problems and implement critical thinking

Students who have grown up following the Montessori approach already know how to think critically and engage in problem-solving discussions. And the college environment is perfect for putting this on a test and further reinforcing it. Self-centered learning is very useful for this aspect because students know how to approach problems analytically and think of different outcomes so they can design their own plans of action. Since the point of this type of learning is to make children responsible for designing a study approach that would bring them the greatest benefit, they can easily succeed because they'll know how to face and resolve different obstacles.

Promoting active learning

Active learning means that children are fully engaged in the learning process. This allows them to retain their knowledge for a longer period and control their level of engagement and participation in the learning process.

Increasing engagement and maintaining motivation

Naturally, when students are free to choose what they'll learn and how they'll do that, you'll notice that they exhibit greater motivation and concentration. And that's the very point of the Montessori approach—to encourage them to work on mastering those fields they're interested in so they'll fully invest in the process. Students who know this and are practicing this self-centered approach feel the need to be more engaged in the learning environment, and their motivation lasts longer. This allows them to take full responsibility for their learning, and at the end of this process, they get a sense of accomplishment. This is also a good example of how the Montessori approach promotes intrinsic motivation with long-lasting, rewarding feelings.

Encouraging individualized learning

The point of this individualized learning is that each student learns and acquires the material at their own pace. This is a very important aspect of Montessori schooling because not every child can learn at the same speed. All children, especially those who have been raised following this approach, know their learning capacity and are able to create and follow a tailored study plan.

The result? A fully-customized college experience that aligns with the needs of each student.

Developing lasting learning skills

The point of Montessori learning isn't just to teach children important information regarding different aspects of life. More importantly, it aims to teach them 'how' they should learn in order to develop life-long learning skills. And this self-centered approach does exactly that. Students who apply this practice during their college years learn how to take responsibility for their own learning. This often results in a tendency to continue their educational venture long after they get their college degree.

Overall, self-centered learning is such an important Montessori skill because it encourages students to focus only on the material they're truly interested in. Moreover, it teaches them to take full responsibility for their learning experience and promotes intrinsic motivation, which is rarely achieved by any other approach.

Suggestions for Incorporating Montessori-Inspired Learning Strategies in College Courses

Now that you've learned how positive an impact the Montessori approach can have if implemented into a student's college experience, it's only logical that I introduce you to a few learning strategies to implement. Have a good look at all of them and think about how you can use them to get the most out of your college course experience.

Take advantage of collaborative learning

Collaborative learning is a popular approach practiced in elementary and high school, but it doesn't mean you can't take advantage of it once you start college. This approach is based on working together as a group to develop different projects and work on assignments. This is a great way for you to present and further improve your communication and interpersonal skills, as these are very important throughout your academic education and once you become a part of the workforce.

Students who engage in collaborative work in an attempt to gain knowledge or solve different issues are proven to be more capable of succeeding in a teamwork environment once they start their careers.

Contribute to creating a positive learning environment

The teacher isn't the only one who can promote a positive learning environment. In fact, students have more power to contribute to this than a single person can. The most important thing you should focus on is studying at a place that promotes a sense of calmness and relaxation. If the classroom doesn't allow this, you can easily implement it while studying on campus or at home.

What you need to pay attention to is to be comfortably seated in a space that's free from clutter and outside distractions. You can also play with the power of lighting and create an environment that best works for your concentration. Personalize the learning space by incorporating items that make you feel comfortable (such as your favorite mug or notebook) and indulge in the positive learning experience you contributed to creating.

Use technology for your own benefit

As you know, technology has become an integral part of our everyday lives to the point when no one can imagine their day without at least having their phone by their side. And despite all the distracting apps and social media posts, you can learn how to use the power of technology to improve your college experience.

When working on a new topic requiring in-depth research, quickly navigate the internet to search for all the information you need. During college, you can use different types of online resources to enhance your learning experience, including videos, tutorials, podcasts, or written content. All these might ease the learning process by providing a more in-depth insight or simply a different approach to your research topic, which might leave a lasting impression.

Practice reflection

Another very important Montessori-inspired approach to learning is to practice reflection. You can easily practice this during your college years by reflecting on what you've learned so far to determine how well you've acquired certain knowledge. There are also many reflection-promoting exercises, such as group discussions or journaling, which you can use for your own benefit. Another beneficial thing you can do is set learning-oriented goals and check your progress. This is probably the easiest way to see how far you've come with your objectives and whether you'll need to change something in your approach to further support your learning experience.

Learn from feedback

Lastly, I strongly encourage you to use other students' or teachers' feedback to see whether you're on a good path to achieving your academic goals. The feedback can also teach you about your strengths or weaknesses you might not have been aware of so you can devise a plan to improve or overcome them. Feedback is also a useful tool for self-reflection, so you can use it to address the previous point I discussed.

Suggestions for Incorporating Montessori-Inspired Principles in Career Exploration and Development

If you've been reading this book from the very beginning, or if you've just paid attention to the first chapters when I talked about the principles of this approach and why it's so praised, you'll be familiar with one of its most important claims—nurturing children to grow into complete, independent adults. One of the main goals of the Montessori approach is to arm children with skills and knowledge they can apply long after they get out of school and college. And reading about this so many times surely made you wonder how exactly one can implement the Montessori skills in real life. And this section is dedicated to answering just that.

The point of you or your child getting a certain degree is to start a career they'll feel content with. But how can they be certain about their chosen career path? The choice of a profession is one of the hardest and most important decisions someone can make, as they'll probably work in the field for quite a long time, if not their whole life. So, students must do well during their career exploration to be confident in their choices. And this is how Montessori can assist in their professional search and development:

Promoting self-discovery

One of the first things that Montessori principles focus on is self-discovery. This means that children are led to explore their interests and curiosities so they can focus on guiding their learning experience toward exploring those. Children who have been self-aware about their likes and interests will find it easier to decide about the career path they'd like to follow. They know how their strengths and values can align with different career paths, and they'll feel more confident in choosing the one they feel will bring the most benefits.

In addition, students who have spent their years of formal education following the Montessori philosophy closely will know how to interpret and learn from their experiences, follow their passions, and try different hobbies. All these give them more insightful knowledge about who they are as individuals, which will later help them choose a career path that aligns with their interests. In addition, they'll be familiar with their strengths and weaknesses, which will also help them choose the profession they'll follow.

This is why self-discovery is so important because it empowers them to take responsibility for their career choice and makes it easier to decide which path they'll follow.

Encouraging hands-on experience

Another important aspect of the Montessori approach is that it provides students with hands-on experience. This is very important when exploring their career options and encouraging further development. One way to use this beneficial approach is to undertake internships and take advantage of different learning opportunities. Combining these will help them gain practical knowledge and develop many useful skills. Moreover, it will also give them a feel of how choosing a different career path will impact them. However, don't expect that following these principles will help you choose the career path of your dreams at first. Although this task will indeed be much easier for you (now that you know your interests and strengths), it doesn't necessarily mean you'll get it right on the first try. So, the opportunities for hands-on experiences will also prove to be very beneficial if you're interested in changing your career orientation and exploring another industry.

Another positive impact of this direct experience is allowing students to develop a professional network before they even get into a certain field. These relationships can be incredibly valuable because they will allow them to gain insider information and learn about potential opportunities in their industry of choice.

Nurturing collaboration and networking

Similar to the benefits of hands-on experience, the overall Montessori teaching aims to nurture as many collaborations with other people as possible. This applies to your school environment when you can work with your peers and in your work or internship when you can communicate with others working in your desired field.

One way to ensure good networking is to apply for an internship or mentorship program that will allow you to connect with professionals who have chosen your dream career path. This will give you a first-hand experience of what your job will look like, and you'll also receive some insightful knowledge from the people you've connected with.

Promoting self-direction

Another one of the core Montessori principles is self-direction. This means that you'll receive the needed skills and knowledge to take responsibility for your career choice and be able to fully rely on your judgment. This will further cause students to develop a sense of individuality and independence over their careers.

Overview of Resources and Support for Montessori-Inspired Learning in College

You've hopefully learned so far that the Montessori approach isn't exclusively reserved for children attending elementary and high school. In fact, these principles are very convenient for broader use, and with a bit of adjustment, you can successfully implement them into your college environment. Montessori-inspired learning in college can be made possible with the use of various resources and support systems.

Here are a few suggestions about different resources you can use to support yourself during the years that lead to you getting your college degree:

Coursework inspired by the Montessori principles

With the knowledge you've gained about how to use the Montessori approach to improve your learning experience throughout college, you can work your way and slightly adjust the coursework material to better align with those principles. What I mean by this is that you can try and implement more self-directed learning, use different resources to enhance your learning experience, and collaborate with fellow students to achieve better academic results. In addition, undertake specific courses that align with your career vision and your personal interests and capabilities to create your own educational path focused on enhancing your strengths.

After all, the Montessori approach aims to reinforce your strengths and direct your education toward your true interests. And the college environment is the ideal place to put this into practice and enroll in courses that will help your academic development.

College communities

Colleges are also where students begin to feel more aware of their involvement in society and different communities. This is why you must become a part of a college community that will allow you to thrive—perhaps one made of other students who wish to continue implementing the Montessori principles into their college learning experience. If there isn't one, maybe you can take the initiative and gather like-minded colleagues to create your learning community. This will allow you to support yourselves during the learning process, share insights and experiences on different topics, and even engage in fruitful debates when discussing how to further enhance your learning experience.

Another benefit of joining or forming such a community is the fact that you'll establish new friendships and networking opportunities. This is something that will help you not only while you're in college but also once you finish your academic education.

Mentors

College teachers can be great mentors in supporting your Montessori learning approach—if they're up for it. They can use their teaching experience and provide additional course materials or resources to help you achieve your academic goals. They can also support you if you're willing to further explore your strengths and interests by giving you different opportunities to test them.

Various learning opportunities

The variety of learning opportunities is another way to implement the Montessori method and further decide about your academic orientation. These can come in the form of different courses, conferences, meetings, internships, and co-op programs, all of which can give you valuable insight and help determine your goals.

Career support

Lastly, you should try to find out whether your college has a career service that helps students explore different career options. The guidance and support these provide won't only assist you in making up your mind about which profession you should ultimately choose but will also better prepare you for the job market you're about to enter a few years from now. Moreover, these services can also give you personalized feedback, different learning and internship opportunities, along with some self-discovery tools that you'll find very useful.

Although many resources and assistance alternatives were probably not created with Montessori principles in mind, you can still modify them to your advantage and achieve satisfactory outcomes. The most important thing is to stay open to the different learning opportunities and take them to gain knowledge and experience you won't only use during college but once you start building your career, too.

Chapter 11:

Montessori-Inspired Parenting of Young Adults (ages 22-25)

I think you would all agree that you can never stop being a parent to your child. No matter whether they're 3, 13, or 23 years of age, your love and care for them never cease. As a parent, you always try to nurture, support, and guide your child onto the right path. If you've brought them up following the Montessori principles, you might be thinking about how far you should go in using those to inspire your parenting approach. And the answer is, why stop, anyway? Montessori principles promote children's holistic and advantageous growth in an environment that gives them complete freedom to follow their interests. And this is something that positively reflects once they become adults.

But is it possible to still take advantage of the Montessori approach once your kids become adults? If you're one of those parents who wonder how to let this philosophy still inspire your parenting approach toward young adults, here you'll discover all you need to know about Montessori parenthood of children aged 22-25.

Addressing the Developmental Needs and Milestones of Young Adults in a Montessori Way

Young adults, i.e., people between 22-25 years, sometimes find themselves confused in the transition between college and adulthood. So, how can you support this change and help them smoothly go through this phase? Here are a few important points you should consider that will help you meet your child's developmental needs into their young adulthood stage.

Promote independence

You should never stop promoting the need for independence, so your parenting approach will primarily need to encourage that. If you've raised your child to follow the Montessori approach, they'll already be generally independent since this philosophy promotes the need to be self-sustainable from the youngest age.

As a parent, what you can do at this point to further promote your child's independence is to get them to take responsibility for their decisions. This will allow them to work on their confidence, resilience, and the feeling of having a purpose in their society. Moreover, you should encourage them to practice being organized by designing their schedules and managing their finances, as this is something that will serve them further in life.

By fostering the need for them to be more independent, take responsibility for their life decisions, and enhance their confidence, you can better prepare your child to deal with adult-life challenges and make the transition between the two periods smoother.

Provide creative opportunities

The next thing you can do as a parent to young adults is to provide them with opportunities for creative thinking. If you've raised them following this approach by now, they're probably already familiar with their interests and abilities. So, why not remind and encourage them to start practicing what they possibly forgot they enjoyed? It may be art, cooking, writing, or any other hobby they used to love when they were little. You might even surprise them by providing the tools required for this creative task.

Furthermore, you can also encourage them to seek out new creative possibilities, perhaps something they haven't tried before but might find appealing now.

Encourage critical thinking

Critical thinking is very important for every adult, and children very close to entering their adult stage should actively practice this invaluable trait. This is yet another feature actively developed if you follow the Montessori principles when raising them from a young age. If, however, you've recently discovered the benefits of this approach, then know that it's not too late to implement it into your parenting strategy now.

You can teach them to challenge their ideas, question their assumptions, and be critical when considering their environment and the world. This will help them develop an awareness and a sense of empathy and make them more capable of making informed decisions related to their current or future work experience.

Nourish their love for learning

Another quality that's very important to promote is the love for learning. This isn't something that has proved to be beneficial during the years of their formal education. In fact, it's a positive feature that will serve them for the rest of their lives, especially now, when they're actively searching for a job or have just entered the workforce. Encourage them to take upon challenges and stay motivated to learn something new from their progressively changing environment, as the practical knowledge they acquire now will serve them for years.

Support their well-being

As parents, you're all concerned about your child's well-being, no matter how independent they've become. At this stage, it's very important to support their physical (especially mental) health by frequently discussing topics that concern them. Pay attention to and discuss how they're dealing with the new challenges in adult life, and support them in any way you can. Remind them to be aware of their well-being, not neglect themselves, and regularly practice self-care.

Explanation of How Montessori Principles Can Be Applied to Living as a Young Adult

The Montessori-based parenting method will be extremely valuable in this transition from student to working and fully responsible adult. Many young adults feel overwhelmed by all the sudden changes that happen once they leave college and begin living adult life. As a parent, it's your responsibility to make this process if you can, and Montessori offers several useful principles that can be applied to their lives.

Following are some examples of how your parenting method that's adapted to their needs will prove to be invaluable in practical life:

Promoting independence

One of the Montessori philosophy's main goals is to raise children with an enhanced sense of independence. This is an important feature of any complete adult capable of thriving in the work and social environment. As a parent of a young adult, it's very important not to stop encouraging your child's independence and find a way to support them without having them think that you'd do the work for them. They should take full responsibility for their lives and decisions, and you can successfully promote them by encouraging them to take charge of their lives and manage their own finances. They need to be confident about what they're capable of, meaning that they should be aware of their strengths and weaknesses, as this is the only way they can become self-sufficient.

Encouraging self-directed learning

Self-directed learning is yet another very important feature you can encourage with your parenting approach. This is where youngsters are taught to take responsibility for their learning process and develop their own agendas and plans on how to achieve a certain educational goal. This doesn't only apply to their formal education but to all the practical knowledge they'll acquire from the social or work environment once they get their college degree. You can play your part by encouraging them to take workshops or courses to further enhance their talents or help them acquire new skills.

Inspiring creativity

I already talked about creativity a few paragraphs ago, but I will tackle this topic again since it's very important. As a parent, you can think of different ways to encourage your child's creativity, which is also applicable during their young adulthood stage. Encourage them to go after their dreams, ideas, and interests even outside their work environment. It's always better to have more skills because they can't possibly know what the future will bring them and when they'll use their creative outlets.

Fostering collaboration

Being able to collaborate with other people is one of the biggest traits of any adult. No person works by themselves both in their learning and work environment, which is why they need to gain a sense of collaboration. Effectively working with other people will promote a thriving teamwork environment where your child can express their opinions and listen to and learn from others. This is very essential for them to thrive in any environment, especially in the workplace.

Teaching critical thinking

Implementing the Montessori philosophy into your parenting approach when guiding your child will promote many positive outcomes. For example, one of the greatest traits a young adult can get is the ability to engage in critical thinking. This is a very important feature that will serve them to make rational decisions, consider many aspects before jumping to conclusions, and research different viewpoints before deciding on their own. This will benefit them in the work environment and as they pace through their lives, as they'll certainly face many situations in which they'll have to use their critical thinking to resolve a certain issue.

Setting goals and time management

From little, kids have their dreams and goals, some of which they meet and some they forget about. However, preparing a child to enter adulthood means they must realize the importance of setting goals and managing their time to work out a plan to help them. With proper guidance, they'll know how to set clear and realistic goals and how to get it all done by working smartly in managing their time.

Taking responsibility

Another important feature of every adult is to be responsible for their decisions, actions, and choices. And this is something that can be made achievable with the application of the Montessori principles to your parenting approach. Being a healthy adult means you can't blame others if something doesn't turn out as planned. You need to encourage your children to be accountable for their lives and all the actions they take.

Promoting respect

Being respectful is yet another essential feature of adults. And this is best taught when children aren't still completely developed. Being a parent of a young adult means you have to remind them to be respectful toward people they interact with daily. Encourage them to look forward to forming healthy relationships with the people around them and, most importantly, treat them with kindness and empathy. Tell them that it's very important to practice effective communication and to be good listeners because these two factors are the keys to forming good relationships with others.

Being responsible for the environment

Just like your child has to be responsible for their own words, actions, and life choices, it's just as important to show respect toward the environment they're living in. Remind them that they directly impact how their environment looks and that even the smallest changes can show great results over time. You can show them how to show greater care about their carbon footprint by teaching them how to recycle and compost, how they can save water and energy, and why they should support environmentally-friendly businesses. This will all greatly impact their knowledge and opinion, as well as the environment.

Discussion of the importance of independence, responsibility, and personal growth in young adulthood

There are many aspects of how a Montessori environment positively affects children's development, including those in the stage of young adulthood. Every parent wants to see their children grow into complete and self-reliant adults, but not all of them know how to contribute to making this happen. Implementing the Montessori approach into their parenting methods is a great way to promote positive values that kids just entering adulthood will use for the rest of their lives.

But what exactly are these good values Montessori promotes, and how can they positively impact their social and work lives?

As a parent, you want your child to grow into a healthy adult who's independent, knows how to take responsibility, and can be in charge of their own personal growth. And this is exactly what using the Montessori principles can help you reach.

Although young adults are almost fully developed grown-ups who have finished or are close to finishing their formal education, they can still learn and change their mindsets.

As a parent, you need to use every opportunity you get to positively influence their stands and assure a complete and healthy development. Teaching your child to be responsible will undoubtedly bring them some of the greatest benefits in life. Knowing that they can't blame others for their own decisions or actions will make them re-think every step and be more calculated when approaching a new area in life. Being responsible also means they'll gain full control over their lives and can navigate their growth in a way they think will benefit them most. In addition, the sense of responsibility will also enhance their sense of self-control, which can prevent unwanted behaviors and potential quarrels with other people.

The next thing young adults should reach is independence, which is no less valuable than the sense of responsibility they should have. If I can say, these go hand in hand because being responsible for your own actions means that you're independent to think and decide for yourself. Young adults will especially benefit from being more independent because this will help them to better handle the transition to adulthood. Being independent will also allow them to be more confident in their strengths and abilities, which will teach them to be more self-reliant regarding other aspects of their lives.

Ultimately, using the Montessori approach to parent young adults will promote their personal growth and inspire them to continue learning long after they get out of their college classrooms. Implementing it in your parenting approach will result in your children showing more interest in pursuing their talents and passions and working on improving themselves. This pursuit of exploring their identities and learning more about their passions will ultimately lead to them gaining a sense of purpose in their society or work environment. And this is undoubtedly a very important attribute any adult can have.

Suggestions for Incorporating Montessori-Inspired Principles in Living as a Young Adult

As you were able to understand by now, Montessori has proven to be an incredibly beneficial approach that provides young adults with essential traits they can use throughout their lives. But, apart from being able to translate this approach into your parenting practice, is there a way to inspire your child to apply Montessori principles in their daily living? Fortunately, there is, and I'm here to provide a few ideas that could inspire positive change in the lives of young adults:

Forming daily routines

Daily routines are one of the most useful activities you can promote that your young adult starts to practice in their lives. Many young people find it hard to navigate through the sudden change in their environment and responsibilities. This can often create a negative and overwhelming feeling that they can't find time to do everything on their schedules. Based on the Montessori method, creating a daily agenda will prove to be very useful. Encourage your child to try and create an agenda that will include time for work, exercise, rest, and other activities they're interested in. This is the most effective way to help them stay organized and manage their work and free time.

Setting goals

Another thing I already mentioned a few points above is setting goals, which you should encourage your child to do. Once they have their dreams and goals written on a piece of paper, they'll be able to look at them and decide how they can make a plan to achieve them all. Ultimately, they can prioritize their goals and even remove some that are very hard to achieve at that point or aren't significant to them. Once they set their goals, you can advise them to break them into simpler and easily-achievable points. This will allow them to track their progress more easily and avoid making them feel overwhelmed if they focus only on a specific goal's outcome.

Embracing learning

A popular saying states that a man learns all his life, a very important thing every young adult must realize. Their quest for gaining knowledge doesn't end once they get their college or university diploma. Many argue that that's the point it begins. You should encourage your child to stay eager for new learning opportunities long after they finish their formal education. They should continue learning in their work and social environment and embrace any new information they come across. Moreover, they should value and caress their love for reading books, taking new courses or workshops, and pursuing hobbies that interest them.

Practicing mindfulness

Another aspect the Montessori philosophy focuses on is the notion of mindfulness. This approach encourages children and young adults to be present in every moment and be aware of their surroundings. If you notice that your child is becoming overpowered by their daily tasks and responsibilities, suggest that they try to incorporate mindful practice into their routines. This can include meditation, yoga, or simply walking in nature—anything that will allow them to fully shift their thoughts to the present moment and experience life.

Creating a motivating working and learning space

No person can work or learn if they do not feel their environment is stimulating. For that reason, it's very important that you advise young adults to pay more attention to the environment they're spending their creative or thoughtful time in. First, based on the Montessori method, having a separate space where they do their work or study is useful. This will provide a feeling that they're supposed to focus solely on their tasks while they're spending time there. In addition, they can customize this environment and make it a motivating space in many ways. They can bring their favorite coffee cup or the notebook they enjoy writing in.

Developing self-awareness

Self-awareness is yet another very important feature in young adults; the Montessori philosophy promotes this from a young age. Everyone should be aware of their strengths and weaknesses so they'll know how to use them to their benefit. This will further make them more capable of making intentional choices and understanding their own thoughts and behaviors.

Practicing empathy

Empathy is, unfortunately, not a feature everyone has mastered, but it's a very important trait of every complete and healthy adult—and one of the basics when it comes to Montessori philosophy. This means showing understanding and appreciation for people who are, perhaps, different from them. But instead of pointing them out, children should be taught to recognize and appreciate the differences. You should guide your children toward showing empathy for other living beings, especially those they encounter daily. This will result in building stronger relationships between one another, which will bring more value into their lives.

Focusing on self-care

But apart from showing care and empathy toward those around them, young adults should also learn how to spend quality time in their presence. As a parent, you should encourage them to pay more attention to self-care and implement different activities to promote this. For example, the Montessori method suggests focusing on preparing healthy meals and dedicating themselves to a wholesome diet, practicing physical activity, or simply relaxing to soothe their senses and rest from all their daily responsibilities.

Taking opportunities for community engagement

Last but not least is the importance of community engagement. All people, especially young adults, will benefit greatly from being exposed to or included in different meetings or activities in social or work communities. You can suggest volunteering, civic engagement, or advocacy, as these will also help them positively impact the environment and give them a sense of purpose.

Overview of Resources and Support for Montessori-Inspired Living for Young Adults

For those of you who are getting familiar with this approach for the first time, you probably find it challenging to properly include all I've mentioned above in your parenting practice. And like with any other topic you're just touching upon, it's good to gain as much insight as possible to properly apply it into practice.

In terms of adapting your parenting approach according to the Montessori principles, you'll find it useful to know different resources that will help you guide your child properly. After all, this is something that would impact their lives, so you'd want to do it right. Have a look at the following resources that will help you support young adults in living their Montessori-inspired lives.

Montessori books

One of the first resources you should rely on is different types of Montessori books that are suitable for the issue you're dealing with. I encourage you to read this one from beginning to end (if you haven't started from the beginning already), as there is plenty of important information to help you gain a deeper understanding of this approach and adapt your parenting techniques according to its principles. You can also turn to literature written by Dr. Montessori and learn from her first-hand insight on this topic.

Online courses and workshops

Another good source of information you'd benefit from is Montessori-inspired online courses and workshops. These often deal with certain topics, such as the one you're interested in discovering—parenting your young adult utilizing the Montessori principles. You can do your own research online and see whether you can find something useful. In addition, there could be some that your child can attend so they can learn something by themselves.

Montessori mentors

Some people offer coaching services that follow the Montessori principles. If you don't feel confident to tackle this topic on your own, you can search for professionals that would make this material easier to comprehend. Moreover, these coaches often offer supervised and personal support to young adults so your child can be directly included in the process.

Communities and organizations

Besides the online courses and mentors, several Montessori-inspired organizations promote a type of living that uses this philosophy's principles. Feel free to research and see whether you can find one in your area so you or your child can use their resources or attend events that would benefit them. In addition, you can form new and positive connections with other people attending their meetings and share your opinions about supporting your child through your Montessori parenting approach.

Podcasts, blogs, and social media

Apart from the many books and courses, the internet is overwhelmed with podcasts, blogs, and social media accounts concerned with this approach. So, during your daily scrolling through Twitter or Instagram, you'll benefit from coming across a post or two about different Montessori aspects. This is a great way to further broaden your knowledge and gain more insight into the topic.

Do your research and follow several accounts that you think will offer you beneficial information and learn from them. Think about how you can implement the things you learn into daily practice and consider how you can improve your parenting approach. Ultimately, it's all about enhancing your parenting practice so your child can benefit from it.

Meet-ups and events

Lastly, you might benefit from knowing there are also several Montessori meet-ups and events you can attend, from which you'll gain invaluable insight into the topic. These events are great for providing various learning and networking opportunities. Use the information you'll gain from attending them and consider how you can implement them into your daily practice of parenting your child into their young adulthood.

By exploring the different resources and support groups, you, as a parent, can see many benefits once you decide to implement those into your parenting technique. The Montessori philosophy provides many beneficial opportunities for children who are just before entering their adulthood stage, so it's crucial you recognize and properly implement them into your guidance.

Chapter 12:
Applying Montessori Principles to Technology Use

Technology has become deeply embedded into our daily lives and routines, so much so that we can't imagine spending a day (some not even an hour) without our phones. We seem to always check our emails and social media inboxes—or simply scroll through our news feeds to see what the community we follow is up to. However, I can't deny the fact that many of you also use it for educational purposes, whether researching a topic or simply verifying information. This has become a part of the daily lives of adults and children, and you probably wonder how beneficial (or harmful) this extent of technology use has become. The concern arises regarding kids using technology as you ask yourself whether this habit has a place in your home Montessori environment.

In this chapter, I will focus on the overall impact of technology on children and teenagers and provide suggestions about applying the Montessori principles during your child's screen time.

Discussion of the Challenges of Technology Use for Children and Teenagers

Being a parent today means that you can totally relate to the information I've shared in the introduction. Technology is, to many, more of a leisure or habit than a convenience, and this can be incredibly unhealthy for young children or teenagers. It has been estimated that some children spend between 8 to 11 hours on the Internet daily! (*Common Sense* Media) This means that they're probably using technology while doing other tasks, such as eating their meals, watching movies, attending school, and even doing their homework or studying. And this can't be beneficial for their health and academic success.

I'm aware that many of you would like to limit your kids' screen time to promote more healthy and active growing and learning. However, that's easier said than done, which probably gets you to think about the following question—how much of an impact technology has on your children?

It's true; we can't discuss the challenges of kids' major exposure to technology without considering the benefits this outlet provides. For example, children can use the power of technology and turn it to their own benefit by using the internet's wealth of information to explore and learn about a certain topic. Moreover, it can also help them develop their multitasking skills, improve their problem-solving skills, and teach them how to be more resourceful when researching. However, leaving your child unattended and giving them unlimited access to a phone or tablet can also have some negative results.

Have a look at the following list, which contains the possible challenges children can face if they're exposed to technology for extended periods:

Lowered attention span

Younger children and teenagers who spend a large portion of their days on their phones or tablets will probably suffer from a decline in their ability to focus on doing one thing for an extended period. Unfortunately, this is one of the first and most noticeable negative effects of technology on children. The main reason is that the internet allows children to get whatever they need whenever they need it. No more waiting for their show to start at a specific time—with a few clicks, they can play it whenever they want. And because of all these instant responses and ready-made entertainment options, kids find it harder to focus on a task for longer.

Declining academic success

Naturally, the inability to focus on doing their tasks or learning will lead to a decline in students' academic success. The increase in technology use will result in children spending less time doing their homework or studying for their exams because they're distracted by looking at their phone screens all the time. In addition, children at the age when they're supposed to be learning how to read and write will find it hard to achieve these skills faster due to their tech exposure.

Difficulties with social interaction

Another negative aspect of children being constantly exposed to technology is their decreased ability to engage in social interactions. Being glued to the screen for a period will make it harder for them to establish face-to-face interactions. Instead, they'll mostly rely on texting or talking using different social media apps instead of preferring to have a conversation in person. Even if they happen to sit together in a room, you may notice that they're spending more time on their phones instead of engaging in a mutual conversation.

Health issues

Despite the social and developmental issues, children who spend much time on their phones, tablets, or computers can also face some health problems. First and foremost, they might develop an unhealthy sitting and standing posture, which can cause pain and discomfort. In addition, because they're spending their free time staring at the screen instead of playing outside, the risk for obesity increases.

Lack of privacy and increased exposure

Lastly, being on the internet means leaving a trail and sensitive personal info. For children who are still not aware of the potential risk, this can be a significant cause for concern. Although cybersecurity is always improving, it's not always perfect. There are still many people out there who can abuse personal info for different purposes. Young children and teenagers often fail to consider this potential risk when leaving their information on different sites on the internet, so you must be aware of this and give your child guidance. They must be made aware of potential predators - older adults pretending to be children, and the importance of never giving out your real name or location. Children and teenagers should be encouraged to avoid inappropriate content and to ask mom or dad for guidance if they have any doubts.

You and I can both agree that it's practically impossible to forbid your child access to technology. Due to the fact that it's been so deeply implemented in every aspect of our lives today, the best you can do is come up with your own approach to limit screen time and familiarize them with the potential risks of technology use. More importantly, you can try to turn this to their own benefit by learning how to apply the Montessori principles to practice.

Explanation of How Montessori Principles Can Be Applied to Technology Use, Especially Screen Time

The Montessori philosophy is based on a holistic approach, which seems to be applicable everywhere. As a parent, you'll find this incredibly helpful, especially if you're dedicated to raising your child following the Montessori principles as closely as possible. After all, you wish to create the perfect thriving environment for your child to grow in, so it's only natural that you'll look for ways to make this happen.

Regarding technology use, I can't say I've ever met a parent who's not concerned about it. Children are starting to spend more and more time on their phones and tablets and less time encouraging genuine conversations or following their interests. To help you develop a good strategy to address this growing problem, I decided to share some useful insight into how you can apply the Montessori principles to technology use and make your children get the most out of their screen time. But before I delve into the details, let's first review what your child needs to reach optimal development.

Children and Teenagers' Developmental Needs

If you've started reading this book from the very beginning, you've noticed that each chapter concerned with different children's ages contains a section that focuses on their developmental needs. Although some of them are exclusive to an individual's age group, many still apply to them all. Feel free to go back to the chapter that discusses your child's age to learn more details about their growing needs, as I'm here to talk about those that affect them all, regardless of their age group.

Every child needs a healthy and thriving environment to reach optimal development, whether they're an infant, preschooler, or teenager. Of course, some of them will vary depending on their age group, but some are universal for all. Things like receiving support and understanding and the freedom to express their thoughts and emotions apply to all children. In addition, attending a beneficial learning environment is another thing every parent should try to give to their kids.

However, when it comes to the use of technology, this can easily alter the idealistic picture. Like all humans, children are meant to communicate and engage in learning by nature. But being glued to the phone screens for a prolonged period can really lower these inborn instincts. No virtual substitutes for real human engagement will satisfy the need for physical interaction, such as playing, collaborating, and communicating in person. Therefore, you need to find ways to limit screen time or turn it into a positive experience and inspire your child to learn and interact in face-to-face conversations and play.

Below, you'll discover a few suggestions for utilizing the Montessori principles and effectively implementing them into technology use.

Building a foundation is key

As I said, children need to spend their time interacting with other kids, expanding their knowledge, discovering their talents, and building important life skills. As a parent, this should be your priority. So, instead of relying on the entertainment technology can bring, you should encourage them to do another engaging activity, such as reading a book.

This will bring so much more value and creative opportunities without any distractions.

However, I'm aware that most of you are concerned about separating your child from the others. If most of their peers have their own phones or know how to use a computer, how will your child learn to do the same in the future if you try to keep them away from technology use now? And although I understand your concern, I must tell you that this kind of thinking is completely unreasonable. Technology is ever-changing, so what your child will learn when they're six will probably not be in use once they turn 16. So, based on the Montessori method, instead of serving your child with effortless entertainment, you should raise them to be motivated learners, critical thinkers, and eager explorers.

Another question you may have is how to deal with your child when they're fussy or restless without the use of technology. I know that letting them watch something on a tablet will keep them calm while you're preparing dinner, but is this really something that will benefit your child? Think about what other parents did in similar situations when there was no such great technology exposure. Of course, times have changed, but genuine forms of entertainment are still more or less the same. So, instead of providing them with a quick fix, encourage your child to read a book, play a game, draw, color, or do something else that will keep them busy while you're doing your household chores. This will amuse them and teach them how to handle strong emotions and entertain themselves.

Prepare the environment

Another important thing you should do is prepare for the environment. Ultimately, kids learn from what they're exposed to, which means that if you don't provide them with many technology-using opportunities, they certainly won't get used to that. As you know, children need a well-prepared and healthy environment promoting holistic growth. This means that you need to focus on creating one that engages their senses, challenges their cognitive abilities, and ultimately teaches them essential life skills. And staring at a motion screen doesn't do much about this issue.

The more time your little one or teenager spends on their electronic gadgets, the less they'll be able to make their own decisions or contribute to their development. And because they're only staring at the screen without moving, this approach ignores an important aspect of the Montessori philosophy—that children experience the greatest advancement when they're indulging in motor and physical activity. This is based on Dr. Montessori's observation that children learn best when provided with hands-on learning opportunities, as there's an important connection between cognition and movement.

Observe before you make decisions

Observation is a very important tool in this approach. In fact, the whole Montessori philosophy is based on observation, as its founder closely watched how kids interacted with their environment and made decisions based on her findings. So, as a parent, you need to learn from her approach and implement it into your parenting method. This means that you should closely observe your child and draw conclusions from what you've been able to see.

Notice whether your child is relaxed, cooperative, alert, restless, impulsive, or easily frustrated. Consider whether there's a link between their behavior and the time they're spending in front of the screen to see whether you should continue with your parenting approach or make some changes and limitations. Given the fact that children are sensorial learners, they're more sensitive to their environment. What doesn't affect you as an adult will probably significantly impact them. Therefore, take notes about how your child behaves or feels after they've been exposed to the use of technology and decide based on what you've observed.

Stick to your goals

One of the most important aims of the Montessori approach is to raise children who are able to stay focused—even when they're surrounded by distractions. In today's world, electronic gadgets are one of the most powerful distractions your child will have to overcome or disregard. If you're designing your parenting approach following the Montessori principles, you'll know that your main goal should be building a sense of intrinsic motivation in your child or teenager. They should know how to stay concentrated and focus on learning despite the challenges from their surrounding. Thus, you must align your decisions with your parenting goals and limit your child's screen time accordingly.

Decide how you'll proceed

There has been plenty of research that proved that technology has a negative impact on children's development. This means you should limit screen time exposure as much as possible to give your children the optimal thriving environment. This applies to children of all ages, including teenagers, as they're all actively developing as individuals.

Students need real-life experiences for as long as they're developing their cognition, learning to control their emotions and impulses, and acquiring new information. Exposing them to unrestricted technology use will not only interfere with this natural process but will also negatively impact it. After all, there are many more beneficial methods to engage your child, which will positively impact their creativity, curiosity, sensorial and congenital development, and so much more. A healthy approach to parenthood should focus on bringing out the best in your child while still allowing them the freedom to follow their interests. So, instead of letting them spend plenty of time in front of their tablet or computer screen, suggest that they read a book, spend some time outdoors, or actively participate in home tasks.

Suggestions for Incorporating Technology in a Montessori-Inspired Way

If you've decided to do everything in your power to create a beneficial growing environment for your child and limit screen time as much as possible, you will need a plan to achieve this. Luckily, you can easily do these by implementing the Montessori philosophies into your parenting approach. So, although you can't completely eliminate technology from your children's lives, there are several things you can do to decrease their use of electronic gadgets. That way, they'll have plenty of time to focus on different aspects of their individuality that will greatly benefit them as they're growing up.

However, don't expect that this is going to be an effortless experience. Including just the right amount of screen exposure into your Montessori-inspired parenting strategy is definitely challenging. The good news is—it's far from impossible. Have a look at the suggestions I've listed below and use them while you design the optimal home setting for your kids.

Promote self-directed learning

One of the greatest benefits of the Montessori approach is that it prepares children for self-directed learning. This means they're developing the ability to recognize their interests and abilities and find proper resources and materials to satisfy their learning needs. Therefore, they can use the power of the internet and technology to research the topics they're interested in, design different projects, and share their work with their peers.

Use technology as a learning tool

Technology can serve as a valid learning tool, but only if students know how to use it. So, instead of using it only for entertainment, they can try different educational apps and interactive tools or research to better understand various concepts and ideas. For example, you can suggest learning about different cultures, discovering music, practicing their language skills, etc. Many Montessori school websites or Montessori-based educational sites share their favorite apps, so finding them shouldn't be a difficult task. But to simplify your task, I've included some popular ones. Some of the best apps aligned with the Montessori method include the following:

1. Montessori Activities
2. Montessori Preschool
3. Montessori Words & Phonics
4. Montessori Maths - Add & Subtract Large Numbers
5. Montessori Numbers - Math Activities for Kids
6. Alpha Writer by Montessorium
7. Ludi App
8. Montessori Primary Box
9. Montessori Crosswords
10. Stamp Game

Explain the benefits of real-life connections

One of the greatest benefits technology can offer is the opportunity for individuals to connect with other people—no matter how far they are. So, instead of relying on technology only for entertainment, encourage your child to use it to connect with their peers or participate in online communities. Of course, you do need to monitor who your child is communicating or associating with online. Fostering independence does not come at the expense of safety.

Encourage collaboration

The Montessori approach promotes cooperation, which means you should motivate your child to make the most out of their use of technology by getting in touch and working with their peers, teachers, or mentors. This would be a great way for them to explore their interests, learn something from others who share their passions, and boost their social and educational development.

Promote independence and responsibility

Other important Montessori goals you should promote in front of your child are independence and responsibility. The philosophy has these two ideals deeply rooted in its teaching, guiding students to grow into fully independent individuals who can take responsibility for their actions and decisions. But how can you promote this goal through technology use?

You can directly include your child in the decision-making process of how much screen time they should be allowed on a daily basis. Work with them to set your goals and expectations and let them take the responsibility for sticking to the agreement without you constantly needing to remind them.

Use the Internet as an explorative outlet

As I mentioned, the internet offers plenty of learning opportunities for those who know how to use it. Motivate your children to use their electronic gadgets to explore topics they're interested in or even use them to deepen their understanding of society and the world.

Teach your child how to be mindful when using different electronic gadgets

Another very important thing you should teach your child is to use technology mindfully. This doesn't only mean that they should respect the screen time restrictions you've set in place but also be very aware of their actions while they're online. Moreover, they should also pay attention to how technology makes them feel by reflecting on their emotions after spending some time using their electronic gadgets. Children, especially teenagers, should be able to identify the possible harmful effects of excessive technology and know when they need to take a break.

Be available

Now, let's shift the focus and suggest how to decrease your child's urge to spend more time on their gadgets than they should. And one of the things you should do is make sure you're available for your children. This means that you should dedicate some time every day to do activities together with them and be present when they're trying to communicate with you. Electronic gadgets shouldn't be something you rely on whenever your child is in need of entertainment, so you must be available for your children.

Suggest other activities

Another thing you can do as a parent is suggest other activities your child can engage in instead of technology. Consult the previous chapters to get inspiration for activities suitable for your child's age and have them try them. It may be an activity they can do by themselves, like arranging a puzzle or playing outside, or it can include their own family and help them spend quality time together. Kids are usually not particularly attracted to technology, but the idea is that it will provide them with the entertainment they need. So, propose another activity instead and engage them in something they will actually benefit from.

Be a role model

Lastly, you can't expect your child to stay away from their phone or tablet if you're spending a large portion of your day staring at yours. Children learn best from examples set by others, and there's no better person they can look up to than you. Try to limit your screen time, or at least don't answer your emails and messages in front of them. You can mute your apps so you're not distracted by the notifications' noises or simply put it in silent mode while spending time with your kids.

Overview of Resources for Technology Use in a Montessori Environment

Being aware of the potential benefits and harms of technology use in children and knowing how to properly promote its use in your created Montessori environment isn't all you need to know. You need to know how you can encourage your child to use their electronic gadgets to their own benefit, and that can be trickier than it initially seems.

This is why you'll benefit from knowing the following resources that will encourage adequate use of technology.

Learning apps and games

As I already mentioned, technology can also be used for educational purposes. One of the ways your children can benefit from it is through the usage of educational games and different apps that offer plenty of learning opportunities. You can encourage them to download or play something related to their interests so they'll make the most of their screen time.

Interactive tools

When it comes to technology, there are several interactive tools that your child can use. Apart from phones and laptops, they can also use tablets, VR headsets, or interactive whiteboards, as all of these can improve their learning experience and make it easier for them to understand new concepts.

Online resources

As you know, electronic gadgets allow fast and easy access to the Internet, a network that provides all kinds of information and communication facilities. Therefore, technology can benefit children if they use it to explore new topics and broaden their knowledge about various issues. There are numerous educational videos, virtual expeditions, and online encyclopedias they can use to deepen their understanding of a certain topic or learn something new.

Opportunities for further development

Participating in various workshops, online courses, and conferences can broaden your child's opportunities for further educational or professional development. This is undoubtedly something that the Montessori approach aims toward, as it's focused on raising children who will explore their interests and work on developing them.

Communities

Lastly, being part of one or several communities is vital for following the Montessori approach. As your child grows up and realizes its importance and part in their school or social community, participating online can largely benefit their development. With careful research, they'll be able to find social media groups, forums, and blogs that deal with the topic they're interested in and that will provide valuable information. In addition, they will extend and elevate their social skills.

As a parent, you can also look for online communities that deal with implementing the Montessori approach in parenting techniques. Thanks to those, you'll be able to gain invaluable knowledge from professional educators and people practicing this approach, as they'll share their experience with all community members.

Chapter 13:
Montessori Approach to Parental Guidance on Sex Education for Children

Sex education is an essential aspect of a child's overall development and well-being. It helps children develop a healthy understanding of their bodies, relationships, and their place in the world. The Montessori approach, known for its child-centered philosophy, extends its principles to sex education as well. Montessori parents strive to create a supportive and open environment for their children, enabling them to explore their questions and curiosities about sex respectfully and age-appropriately. This chapter explores how Montessori parents approach sex education, emphasizing the significance of fostering communication, respecting the child's autonomy, and promoting a comprehensive understanding of sexuality.

Creating a Foundation of Open Communication:

Montessori parents understand the importance of establishing open lines of communication with their children from an early age. This foundation of trust and openness allows for discussions about various topics, including sex, to occur naturally. Parents create a safe space for their children to express their thoughts, concerns, and questions. Regular conversations about the body, boundaries, and emotions lay the groundwork for addressing more complex subjects later on.

Respecting the Child's Autonomy:

Montessori parents recognize that children have unique development timelines and individual curiosities. They respect their child's autonomy by allowing them to initiate discussions about sex, ensuring they set the pace and direction of these conversations. Rather than imposing information, parents adopt a responsive approach, actively listening to their child's queries and providing age-appropriate, factual, and honest responses. This approach empowers children to take an active role in their own learning and fosters a sense of ownership over their bodies.

Age-Appropriate Learning

Montessori parents understand that sex education is a lifelong journey that begins in early childhood. They approach it in a developmentally appropriate manner, recognizing that children's understanding of sex evolves as they grow. In the early years, discussions may revolve around body parts, personal hygiene, consent, and understanding basic concepts such as privacy and boundaries. As children enter adolescence, topics such as puberty, reproduction, relationships, and safe sex become more relevant. Montessori parents ensure that the information provided aligns with their child's age, maturity, and level of understanding.

Using Concrete Materials and Visual Aids

Montessori education emphasizes hands-on learning and the use of concrete materials to facilitate understanding. Similarly, Montessori parents utilize age-appropriate visual aids and books to help explain concepts related to sex and sexuality. These materials, designed specifically for children, present information clearly and non-threateningly, using illustrations and age-appropriate language. Such materials encourage exploration and provide children with tangible tools to understand their bodies and the changes they experience.

Incorporating Montessori Values Into Sex Education

Montessori parents integrate the principles of respect, empathy, and responsibility into sex education. They teach their children about consent, healthy relationships, and the importance of treating others with kindness and empathy. Montessori parents lay the groundwork for developing healthy relationships and promoting mutual understanding and respect by emphasizing the importance of personal boundaries and respecting others' boundaries. Try to avoid confrontation with your partner in front of your child if you know it will not be modeling healthy behavior. Try your best to decrease tension in the household and model love. Your mental health is extremely important in how successful your relationships will be with other adults, so please take care of yourself to show your kids what healthy relationships can look like.

If you're in a difficult or dangerous situation, reaching out for help can be the smartest decision you'll ever make for your emotional health and that of your child. This is probably the most difficult guidance I'm giving in the book, but I think it's one of the most important. I have had my share of relationship struggles in front of my children. It was hard not to let my rage out many times. Concern for my children helped me to do my best in establishing peace in the home as best as I was able with the resources I had at the time.

Emphasizing Emotional Intelligence

Sex education within the Montessori framework includes an emphasis on emotional intelligence. Parents discuss the importance of recognizing and expressing emotions, both their own and others'. Children are encouraged to understand and manage their feelings in healthy ways. This emotional foundation is crucial when addressing topics such as consent, body image, peer pressure, and decision-making.

Addressing Values and Cultural Context

Montessori parents understand the significance of discussing values and cultural perspectives regarding sex education. They acknowledge that families may hold different beliefs and values and approach these discussions with sensitivity and respect. Montessori parents engage in conversations that explore diverse perspectives on sex and relationships, helping their children understand that societal norms and cultural contexts influence individual beliefs. By fostering open-mindedness and critical thinking, they encourage their children to form their own values while appreciating the diversity of opinions.

Promoting Healthy Body Image and Self-Esteem

Montessori parents understand that a positive body image and self-esteem are integral to a child's overall well-being. They encourage open discussions about body image, emphasizing that everyone's body is unique and normal. They actively work to promote self-acceptance, self-care, and self-respect rather than body shaming or negative self-talk. Montessori parents teach their children to appreciate their bodies, emphasizing the importance of self-care through healthy habits and fostering a positive attitude toward their physical selves.

Encouraging Critical Thinking and Media Literacy

In today's digital age, Montessori parents recognize the importance of teaching children how to navigate media representations of sex and relationships critically. They engage in conversations about media literacy, helping children understand the difference between realistic portrayals and idealized or harmful depictions. By encouraging critical thinking, Montessori parents empower their children to question and analyze media messages, promoting a healthy skepticism that guards against unrealistic expectations or negative influences.

Addressing Consent and Boundaries

Consent is a crucial aspect of healthy relationships, and Montessori parents prioritize teaching their children about boundaries and consent from an early age. They teach children the importance of respecting personal boundaries and seeking consent before engaging in physical interactions. Montessori parents use age-appropriate language and examples to explain the concept of consent, emphasizing that it applies to all aspects of life, from physical touch to sharing personal information online.

For young children, it's essential to start with age-appropriate discussions that emphasize personal boundaries and bodily autonomy. Parents and educators can use simple scenarios to explain consent, such as asking a child if they'd like a hug or a high-five before giving physical affection. By respecting a child's choice and teaching them that it's okay to say "no" when they're uncomfortable, we lay the foundation for understanding consent as a fundamental aspect of mutual respect.

As children transition into their teenage years, the concept of consent takes on greater significance, especially in the context of romantic relationships. Discussions about consent should encompass more complex scenarios, such as emphasizing the necessity of affirmative and enthusiastic consent in sexual situations. Teens should be encouraged to communicate openly about their boundaries and desires with their partners.

They should understand that consent can be withdrawn at any time.

They should understand consent has nothing to do with what a person is wearing or how they are behaving. Consent should be explicit and re-confirmed. Role-playing exercises can help teenagers practice communication and recognize the importance of seeking and respecting consent. By providing them with knowledge and tools to navigate these conversations, we empower young people to build healthy, respectful relationships that prioritize consent and mutual understanding, ultimately contributing to a safer and more equitable society.

Collaborating with the Montessori Community

Montessori education places great importance on community involvement and collaboration. Montessori parents understand the benefit of working with teachers, administrators, and other parents to reinforce consistent messages about sex education. They actively participate in school initiatives and workshops focused on sex education, providing opportunities for parents to share experiences, seek guidance, and learn from one another. This collaborative approach ensures a comprehensive and unified approach to sex education within the Montessori community.

Conclusion

Montessori parents adopt a child-centered approach to sex education, creating an environment that fosters open communication, respect for autonomy, and age-appropriate learning. By addressing sex education through a Montessori lens, parents empower their children to develop a comprehensive understanding of their bodies, relationships, and sexuality. Through open discussions, age-appropriate materials, and a focus on values, cultural context, and emotional intelligence, Montessori parents equip their children with the knowledge and skills necessary to navigate healthy relationships, make informed decisions, and develop a positive and respectful attitude toward their own bodies and the bodies of others.

Chapter 14: Navigating Gender Identity and Sexual Orientation: Montessori Parents' Approach

Gender identity and sexual orientation are important aspects of human diversity and personal identity. Montessori parents recognize the significance of creating a supportive and inclusive environment where children can explore and understand gender identity and sexual orientation. By fostering open communication, promoting empathy and acceptance, providing age-appropriate education, and offering resources, Montessori parents navigate the topic of gender identity and sexual orientation sensitively and inclusively. This article explores the Montessori parents' approach to navigating gender identity and sexual orientation. It focuses on fostering understanding, embracing diversity, and creating a safe space for children to explore and express their authentic selves.

Establishing a Safe and Inclusive Environment

Montessori parents create an environment that embraces diversity and promotes acceptance. They cultivate a culture of respect where children feel safe to express their thoughts, feelings, and questions about gender identity and sexual orientation. Montessori parents encourage children to explore their identities authentically by providing an open and non-judgmental space. It goes without saying that even when your children are young, avoid derogatory slang and be mindful of the words you use to describe families and relationships.

Fostering Open Communication

Montessori parents initiate open and age-appropriate discussions about gender identity and sexual orientation. They encourage children to ask questions, express their feelings, and share their experiences. By actively listening and responding with empathy, parents demonstrate their commitment to understanding their child's perspective and creating a safe space for dialogue.

Teaching younger children and teenagers about fostering communication regarding gender identity and sexual orientation at home is an intimate and crucial endeavor.

Begin by cultivating an open and accepting environment where your children feel comfortable expressing their thoughts and questions. Actively listen to them without judgment and encourage them to ask about anything they're curious about, including topics related to gender and sexual orientation. This approach helps create a safe space where children and teens know they can approach you with their concerns and seek understanding.

For younger children, consider incorporating diverse media into your home environment. Watch TV shows, movies, or documentaries that feature characters or stories with various gender identities and sexual orientations. Use these opportunities to initiate conversations and explore the different aspects of these identities. Additionally, consider attending local community events, workshops, or support groups that focus on diversity and inclusion. Engaging in these activities together as a family provides valuable learning experiences and reinforces the message that you support and value everyone, regardless of their gender identity or sexual orientation.

Age-Appropriate Education

Montessori parents provide age-appropriate education on gender identity and sexual orientation. They adapt their discussions and resources to suit their child's developmental stage. For younger children, parents introduce the concept of gender diversity and acceptance, while older children receive more comprehensive information about sexual orientation and the LGBTQ+ community.

For younger children, start by introducing the concept of diversity and differences in a positive and age-appropriate manner. Storybooks, for example, can be a powerful tool to teach empathy and respect. Select books that feature characters with diverse gender identities and family structures and use these stories to discuss different experiences. Encourage questions and provide clear, simple answers to help children understand that people can have various gender identities and orientations, which is perfectly normal.

As children transition into their teenage years, it becomes crucial to provide them with accurate information about gender and sexual diversity. Schools and community organizations can play a pivotal role by offering comprehensive sexual education programs that include discussions on gender identity, sexual orientation, and the importance of respecting individual choices. Ensure that these programs are inclusive, affirming, and free from bias or stereotypes. Also, it is vital to foster open dialogues where teenagers can share their thoughts and questions without fear of judgment. Encourage participation in peer-led initiatives, such as LGBTQ+ support groups or diversity clubs, which can provide a safe space for teenagers to connect, learn, and challenge stereotypes. By promoting understanding and acceptance from an early age and continuing these discussions throughout adolescence, we can help create a more inclusive society where everyone is valued and respected for who they are.

Teaching Respect and Empathy

Montessori parents emphasize the importance of respect and empathy in understanding and embracing diverse gender identities and sexual orientations. They teach their children to treat others with kindness, regardless of their gender identity or sexual orientation. Through age-appropriate discussions, parents help children develop empathy by encouraging them to consider the experiences and feelings of individuals who may be different from them.

Engaging in meaningful activities can effectively instill respect and empathy in children and teenagers. Simple activities like role-playing scenarios can be a valuable tool for younger children. Encourage them to take on different roles and perspectives, allowing them to understand how others might feel in various situations. For instance, you can create scenarios where they play both the person who wants to share a toy and the one who has to share it. This hands-on approach helps children recognize the emotions of others and fosters empathy by allowing them to walk in someone else's shoes, promoting a deeper understanding of feelings and needs.

Teenagers can benefit from activities that involve community service or volunteering. Encourage them to participate in initiatives that serve those less fortunate or in need. Whether it's volunteering at a local shelter, organizing a community cleanup, or visiting nursing homes, these experiences teach teenagers the importance of empathy and respect for others from diverse backgrounds and circumstances. Additionally, engage in open discussions about real-world issues and encourage them to voice their opinions while actively listening to their peers. This helps them develop respect for differing viewpoints and promotes critical thinking and understanding of complex social dynamics.

Addressing Stereotypes and Bias

Montessori parents actively challenge stereotypes and biases related to gender identity and sexual orientation. They engage in discussions about gender roles and expectations, highlighting that individuals should be free to express themselves authentically, regardless of societal norms. Parents provide examples of diverse role models and encourage their children to question and challenge stereotypes they encounter.

Using Inclusive Language

Montessori parents model inclusive language by using gender-neutral terms when appropriate and by respecting individuals' preferred pronouns. They explain the importance of using inclusive language in creating an environment where everyone feels seen, valued, and respected.

Seeking Outside Resources and Support

Montessori parents understand the value of seeking outside resources and support to navigate conversations about gender identity and sexual orientation. They engage with books, documentaries, and websites that provide accurate and age-appropriate information. Parents may also connect with LGBTQ+ organizations, counselors, or experts in the field to gain insights and support.

Encouraging Self-Exploration and Expression

Montessori parents encourage children to explore their own gender identities and expressions. They provide opportunities for self-reflection, creative expression, and personal exploration. Parents support their child's self-discovery journey, offering encouragement and understanding along the way.

Creating a Supportive Community

Montessori parents foster a sense of community by connecting with other families and educators who are supportive of gender diversity and sexual orientation. They actively seek out inclusive resources, events, and organizations that provide a support network for their children and themselves.

Emphasize the Value of Love and Acceptance

Montessori parents emphasize that love and acceptance are fundamental values when navigating gender identity and sexual orientation. They teach their children that everyone deserves to be loved, respected, and accepted for who they are, regardless of their gender identity or sexual orientation. By modeling and reinforcing these values, Montessori parents create a foundation for inclusive and accepting attitudes toward all individuals.

Encouraging Advocacy and Allyship

Montessori parents empower their children to become advocates and allies for gender diversity and LGBTQ+ rights. They teach children the importance of standing up against discrimination and supporting those facing challenges due to their gender identity or sexual orientation. Parents guide their children in finding age-appropriate ways to contribute to creating a more inclusive and equitable society.

Celebrating Diversity

Montessori parents celebrate the diversity of gender identities and sexual orientations within their family, community, and the broader world. They expose their children to stories, artwork, and cultural expressions that highlight the richness of diverse identities and experiences. By celebrating diversity, Montessori parents help their children appreciate the beauty and strength that comes from embracing differences.

Conclusion

Montessori parents take a proactive and inclusive approach to navigating gender identity and sexual orientation. By establishing a safe and inclusive environment, fostering open communication, providing age-appropriate education, and promoting respect, empathy, and acceptance, Montessori parents create a supportive space for children to explore and express their authentic selves. Through age-appropriate discussions, modeling inclusive language and behaviors, seeking outside resources and support, and emphasizing love and acceptance, Montessori parents guide their children toward a deeper understanding of gender diversity and sexual orientation. In doing so, they cultivate a culture of respect, empathy, and inclusivity, contributing to a more compassionate and equitable society for all.

Chapter 15: Montessori Parents' Approach to Teaching Kids About Drug and Alcohol Abuse: Age-Appropriate Discussions, Activities, and Resources

Introduction

Drug and alcohol abuse prevention is critical to a child's overall well-being and development. Montessori parents understand the importance of addressing this topic thoughtfully and age-appropriately. They strive to create a supportive environment where open communication, education, and the development of critical thinking skills empower children to make informed decisions. This article explores a Montessori parents' approach to teaching kids about drug and alcohol abuse, providing specific age-appropriate discussions, activities, and resources to foster understanding and promote healthy choices.

Early Childhood (Ages 3-6)

In the early years, the focus was on building a foundation of understanding and providing children with basic information. Montessori parents approach the topic of drug and alcohol abuse by:

- Teaching Body Awareness: Parents introduce discussions on the importance of keeping their bodies healthy and strong. They discuss the effects of healthy habits like exercise, nutritious food, and proper rest, emphasizing that these choices contribute to overall well-being.
- Exploring Medicines: Parents discuss the purpose of medicines and how they help when someone is sick. They teach children the importance of taking medicines only under the guidance of a trusted adult and never consuming medicines without permission.
- Identifying Trusted Adults: Montessori parents emphasize the importance of identifying trusted adults in their lives, such as parents, teachers, or caregivers. They explain that these individuals are there to provide guidance, answer questions, and keep children safe.

Early Elementary (Ages 6-9)

As children grow, Montessori parents continue the discussion on drug and alcohol abuse, providing more detailed information and fostering critical thinking skills. They engage children through the following activities:

- Understanding Medications: Parents explain the difference between prescription medications and over-the-counter drugs. They discuss the importance of following dosage instructions, reading labels carefully, and never taking medications not meant for them.
- Teaching about Harmful Substances: Parents introduce the concept of harmful substances and provide examples such as tobacco, alcohol, and illegal drugs. They explain the potential dangers and negative effects these substances can have on the body and overall health.
- Developing Refusal Skills: Montessori parents help children develop assertiveness and refusal skills. They role-play different scenarios where children are offered substances and teach them how to say no confidently and seek help from a trusted adult.

- Promoting Healthy Coping Strategies: Parents teach children about healthy coping strategies for managing stress, such as engaging in physical activity, spending time in nature, practicing mindfulness, or talking to trusted adults. They emphasize the importance of finding positive outlets for emotions and stress rather than turning to harmful substances.

Late Elementary (Ages 9-12)

In the later elementary years, Montessori parents deepen the discussion on drug and alcohol abuse, addressing peer pressure and providing more comprehensive information. They incorporate the following activities:

- Peer Pressure Discussions: Parents initiate conversations about peer pressure and its influence on decision-making. They discuss ways to recognize and navigate peer pressure situations, including how to choose friends who support healthy choices.
- Educating about Addiction: Parents introduce the concept of addiction and its impact on individuals and families. They explain that addiction is a disease and emphasize the importance of empathy and support for those struggling with addiction.

- Promoting Media Literacy: Montessori parents encourage children to critically analyze media portrayals of substance use. They discuss how advertisements, movies, and social media can influence perceptions and shape behaviors. Parents guide children to question media messages and think critically about the consequences of substance abuse.
- Engaging in Community Initiatives: Parents involve children in community initiatives and activities that raise awareness about drug and alcohol abuse. They may participate in local campaigns, volunteer at substance abuse prevention organizations, or organize awareness events within their community. These experiences provide real-world context and a sense of active involvement in addressing the issue.

Early Adolescence (Ages 12-15)

During early adolescence, Montessori parents focus on building a comprehensive understanding of the consequences of drug and alcohol abuse, promoting responsible decision-making, and providing resources for support. They engage adolescents through the following strategies:

- Comprehensive Education: Parents provide accurate and detailed information about various substances, including their physical and mental health effects. They discuss short-term and long-term consequences, addiction risks, and the impact of substance abuse on relationships and academic performance.
- Discussing Peer Influence: Montessori parents facilitate open discussions about the influence of peers on substance use. They encourage adolescents to critically evaluate their social circles and make choices that align with their values and goals.
- Role-Playing Scenarios: Parents engage adolescents in role-playing scenarios that simulate real-life situations involving drugs and alcohol. This helps develop decision-making skills, assertiveness, and effective communication strategies to navigate challenging situations.
- Exploring Support Systems: Montessori parents introduce the concept of support systems, including counselors, helplines, and support groups. They provide information about resources adolescents can access when seeking help for themselves or for friends who may be struggling with substance abuse.

- Empowering Responsible Choices: Parents emphasize the importance of personal responsibility and making informed decisions. They encourage adolescents to set personal boundaries, establish healthy habits, and resist peer pressure through open communication and assertiveness.
- Engaging in Service Projects: Montessori parents encourage adolescents to actively participate in community service projects related to substance abuse prevention. They may collaborate with local organizations, raise awareness through creative initiatives, or organize educational workshops for younger children.

Late Adolescence (Ages 15+)

During the late adolescence stage, Montessori parents continue to reinforce the knowledge and skills acquired in earlier years while addressing the unique challenges and responsibilities faced by older teenagers. They employ the following strategies:

- In-depth Understanding of Addiction: Montessori parents provide a deeper understanding of addiction as a complex neurological and psychological condition. They discuss the genetic and environmental factors that contribute to addiction, the impact of substance abuse on brain development, and the cycle of addiction.

- Critical Thinking and Decision-Making: Parents engage adolescents in discussions that encourage critical thinking, ethical decision-making, and responsible choices. They explore real-life scenarios, helping teenagers understand the potential consequences of substance use and the importance of considering long-term goals and personal values.
- Exploring Healthy Coping Mechanisms: Montessori parents emphasize the importance of developing healthy coping mechanisms for managing stress and emotions. They encourage adolescents to explore activities such as sports, creative arts, mindfulness practices, or volunteer work as alternatives to substance use.
- Discussing Consent and Peer Pressure: Parents facilitate conversations about consent, healthy boundaries, and assertiveness in navigating peer pressure situations related to substance use. They help adolescents recognize and respect personal boundaries and empower them to make choices

aligned with their values, even in challenging social environments.

- Responsible Party and Social Hosting: Montessori parents discuss the legal and ethical responsibilities related to hosting social gatherings and parties. They emphasize the importance of providing a safe and substance-free environment and the potential consequences of underage drinking or drug use.
- Engaging in Advocacy: Montessori parents encourage adolescents to become advocates for substance abuse prevention within their communities. They support and guide teenagers in organizing awareness campaigns, participating in local policy discussions, or volunteering with organizations dedicated to substance abuse prevention and support.
- Encouraging Lifelong Learning: Montessori parents emphasize that learning about drug and alcohol abuse is an ongoing process. They encourage adolescents to seek reliable resources, books, documentaries, and educational websites that provide updated information and research on substance abuse, addiction, and recovery.

- Building Resilience and Support Systems: Montessori parents emphasize the importance of building resilience and a strong support system. They encourage adolescents to cultivate positive relationships, seek guidance from trusted adults, and foster connections with peers who prioritize healthy choices.

Conclusion

Montessori parents approach the topic of drug and alcohol abuse prevention with a holistic perspective, combining education, open communication, critical thinking, and community involvement. By providing age-appropriate discussions, engaging activities, and access to resources, they empower children to make informed decisions, develop resilience, and navigate the challenges of adolescence. Montessori's emphasis on independence, self-awareness, and empathy enables children to understand the potential risks associated with substance abuse and equips them with the tools necessary to lead healthy and fulfilling lives.

Chapter 16:
Mental Health Benefits

We all want our children to grow healthy in every possible aspect, including the mentally. Therefore, we wish to create the best possible environment for their development, which is why you are reading this book. The Montessori method provides the ideal basis for your child's growth at every possible level, and because it is founded on the *'I learn at my own pace'* principle, without severe punishments and shouting, there are no strains or anxiety as they progress.

In essence, there are many mental benefits associated with the Montessori philosophy. So, below, I will describe how and why this revolutionary principle can both promote good mental health and help you deal with depression and anxiety in both younger and older children.

The list of referenced studies is by no means exhaustive, as this chapter is not meant to act as a systematic review of the literature but rather to provide some data on Montessori-focused research. And, of course, the content provided in this chapter is intended for educational purposes only. It is not a substitute for professional medical advice, diagnosis, or treatment.

Always consult a qualified healthcare provider or physician regarding any specific questions or concerns about your child's health or well-being.

Evidence for the Montessori Method Promoting Good Mental Health Outcomes

Even though I will speak from my own experience, I will dedicate this part of the chapter to studies and research that can back any claim related to the Montessori method.

One thing that led you to read my book is the numerous testimonies over the years that speak of so many positive outcomes regarding children's growth and development. And many of them are particularly associated with mental health. How? Let's explore various examples of what your children can gain from the Montessori method and how it will help them with various mental challenges.

Sense of autonomy and self-esteem through self-directed learning

Because the Montessori philosophy encourages children to simply follow what interests them, they feel more at ease to indulge in self-directed learning. Furthermore, the fact that they can easily explore their environment at their own pace is a huge factor in shaping them as individuals. They can clearly define what interests them, resulting in a sense of autonomy and building their self-esteem, which is very important for nurturing their mental health. In fact, numerous cases where children were raised and taught with the help of the Montessori philosophy have shown high self-esteem levels. But what is more, they have also shown increased motivation and undivided interest—which is another essential aspect for growing into a mentally evolved adult. (Lillard & Else-Quest, 2006; Rathunde & Csikszentmihalyi, 2005).

Reduced stress and anxiety by thriving in a safe and supportive environment

Naturally, as parents, you want your children to feel safe and supported instead of stressed and anxious. The Montessori method is all about creating a harmonious environment where they will thrive by feeling perfectly safe and supported by everyone. In this way, they can indulge in more social interactions, develop a sense of how to cooperate with other children, and, most importantly, they will discover the meaning of a community. So how can this benefit them? According to numerous studies, when children feel safe and motivated to interact, they don't feel as stressed and anxious as those raised and taught in traditional settings. (Dohrmann et al., 2007; Lillard, 2013).

Reduced depression and anxiety as a result of hands-on learning

As you are well aware by now, one of the key approaches of the Montessori method is hands-on learning through practical life skills. As children develop more skills that will serve them in life, they become more independent and self-reliant. Furthermore, this is especially vital for improving their problem-solving abilities and, of course – their motor skills. We've already established how important this is for their academic advancement, but did you know that this also helps them shape their mental health? According to research, those children whose minds have been nurtured with the Montessori philosophy have shown fewer symptoms of anxiety and depression – thanks to practical skills and hands-on learning. (Greenberg et al., 2003).

Reduced depression and anxiety as a result of a child-centered approach

When you have someone who encourages and supports you as a guide – be it a parent or a teacher; instead of serving as an authority, respect and trust are born. With gentle mentoring, the child feels more at ease and is willing to learn and explore more. An interesting study shows that children who see their parents and teachers as caring and supportive figures will have excellent mental health outcomes. Plus, as a result, they end up having fewer symptoms of anxiety and depression. (Hughes & Kwok, 2007)

Higher self-regulation and independence

When you apply the Montessori method, you need to promote these two traits because they lead to an amazing sense of self-efficacy. In this way, children are taught to be responsible for their choices, problem-solving, learning pace, and interests, leading to autonomy, confidence, and elevated mental health both in childhood and adulthood. (Ryan & Deci, 2000).

Higher self-discipline

We already discussed the effect of positive discipline, but it also affects the child's mental health. When children are disciplined via the Montessori method, they become self-disciplined and can have more self-control over various situations. This ability makes them realize they have the power to define boundaries. Of course, these healthy limits help protect them from negative influences, preserving their mental health. (Dogru, 2015)

Reduced depression as a result of integrated curriculum and playful learning

The Montessori philosophy involves allowing children to learn how to make a connection to various areas and develop connections between each of them playfully. It is a holistic view that awakens their curiosity about the world. When they grow interests and interconnect subjects from an early age, they remain motivated to explore even further in life and simply stay interested in the world's wonders. Research shows that this playful learning positively affects their mental health, cultivates more joy, and increases their sensory motor skills. (Panksepp)

Elevated mental health by emphasizing social and emotional development

When you care for and nurture your child's emotional and social side, you are already shaping a healthy individual. And that's what the Montessori method is all about. It gives children a fantastic opportunity to interact with their surrounding peers and even develop a sense of empathy. These positive connections also result in having an understanding of all those in their environment. Of course, these social and emotional skills are the basis for a healthy mentality in kids and adults. (Schonert-Reichl et al., 2015)

Elevated mental health by promoting a connection with nature

It is a well-known fact that the Montessori approach strongly believes in nature-based learning and skill development. Allowing children to spend time in nature makes them feel more relaxed and curious. In turn, this lowers any symptoms of anxiety and stress.

Strategies for Dealing With Anxiety and Depression in Younger Children

Younger children can be affected by anxiety and depression, especially if their environment doesn't promote their individual growth. For any parent, this may seem discouraging, but luckily, the Montessori philosophy has the right answer to deal with this—in a creative way that won't put pressure on any side.

The Montessori method focuses on play, exploration, various sensory activities, mindfulness, positive reinforcement, emotional vocabulary, creative expressions, and more. With its help, your young child will feel more confident, capable, and even more grounded. This is especially vital for dealing with anxiety and depression. Without further ado, here's how you can help your child manage any mental health challenges:

Provide Montessori Sensory Activities

In essence, younger children use their senses when it comes to learning, so offering them a hands-on approach where they can engage in various sensory activities will be greatly beneficial – especially for anxiety. This can include exploring different shapes, colors, and textures. How does this work? These Montessori sensory activities are perfect for making children become present at the moment and grounded, thus helping them deal with anxiety.

Learning through Play and Exploration

Any child loves to play and explore, especially younger ones. But instead of forcing anything, allow them to do it at their own pace and explore their environment. The Montessori method encourages imaginative play, allowing everything to be a child-led learning process. By exploring and playing, they will feel joyful, capable, and in control over their learning pace. In turn, this can alleviate any symptoms of depression.

Put an emphasis on their Emotional Vocabulary

Naturally, younger children don't have a complete or clear understanding of their emotions. Therefore, you can help them identify their feelings. As you've gathered, the Montessori philosophy is based on this approach because it is vital to understand and acknowledge their feelings. I have discussed this for every age, so employ those principles and teach your child to communicate their feelings of anxiety and depression.

Use Positive Reinforcement

Even though positive reinforcement is a pillar for the growth of any age, the Montessori philosophy embraces its importance for younger children and depressive thoughts. Positively nurturing your child's mental health and acknowledging its accomplishments will boost self-esteem and confidence. These two are incredibly beneficial for tackling any depression symptoms.

Encourage Mindfulness through Movement

While traditional mindfulness exercises can be challenging for younger children to practice, the Montessori method provides an alternative. Why not do it through movement? For instance, they can focus on their breathing with the help of yoga poses, dancing, etc. Becoming more mindful will help them feel calmer, more grounded, and in tune with their emotions, thus helping them manage their anxiety.

Give them a Choice

It is no secret that younger children may feel depressed or anxious when they don't have control over their environment. The Montessori philosophy revolves around giving them choices for different activities. This can start with providing an option of which activity to choose, where to sit, what materials they would use, etc. In this way, you are empowering them, reducing any anxious feelings.

Provide them with Opportunities for Movement

As you know, younger children are filled with lots and lots of energy, meaning it can be challenging for them to stay still. However, the Montessori method has a solution: combining physical activity with learning. So, instead of standing still, they can engage in movement such as outdoor play, dancing, yoga, etc. It is a wonderful way to help them regulate their emotions and get rid of depressing or anxious thoughts.

Encourage them to embrace Creative Expression

Creativity is highly regarded in Montessori philosophy—and for a good reason! Think about it: when you allow your young child to express through music, art, or anything else, you are awakening its abilities to process emotions and translate them into those activities. When they unleash some of the anxiety and depression through these creative expressions, the battle is already won.

Having a Quiet Space can work wonders

Sometimes, the answer is some peace and quiet. This is quite understandable when it comes to younger children because they can often get overstimulated in noisy surroundings. Therefore, the Montessori approach suggests providing them with a quiet space to have a break. This helps manage their anxiety, especially if there is also a cozy spot in the room. You can place some soft pillows to make it more soothing.

Strategies for Dealing with Anxiety and Depression in Older Children

Although many of the Montessori method suggestions for managing anxiety and depression in younger children can also apply to older ones, some crucial differences in development require a more personalized and specific approach. Let's go through them.

Encourage Self-Reflection

The Montessori philosophy is deeply rooted in self-reflection as a means for the child to tackle their interests and emotions. So, when dealing with these challenging feelings, self-reflection will prove to be a fantastic tool. As they are older now and more focused, they can engage in various activities like mindfulness practices, meditation, and one of the simplest yet most effective ones – journaling. By understanding where anxiety and depression come from, they can deal with them more easily.

Provide plenty of Opportunities for Independence

Now that you have in-depth knowledge of the Montessori method, you know independence is highly valued. Therefore, ensure your older child has many opportunities to become more responsible for their own learning. This can include allowing them to work independently, set their own goals, pick materials of their choice, etc. What this promotes is being more in control of their surroundings. As a result, you will see that they will become less anxious or depressed.

Encourage them to engage in Group Activities

Even though this might seem obvious, it is another of the fundaments of the Montessori method that can be easily overlooked. Collaboration and having a sense of community are vital for overcoming mental challenges. So, make them see the importance of this by encouraging them to engage in group activities—you will notice how they will feel more connected to others. This will help them battle any depressive emotions and feelings of isolation.

Provide Meaningful and Purposeful Activities

Older children are now more aware of what engaging in meaningful work means and getting a sense of higher accomplishment. That is why it is crucial to involve them in some kind of meaningful work. For example, based on the Montessori method, you can inspire them to choose some community service with the aim of addressing social justice issues. With this, they will get a sense of purpose, fulfillment, and being helpful to the community. These are all rewarding emotions that will help them manage their depression.

Mindful Movement as a tool against anxiety and depression

As I mentioned, some mindful movement principles for younger children can indeed be applied to older ones, but a bit differently. For example, now that your child has more developed learning abilities, it is time to move to something else, like practicing tai chi, qigong, and yoga. All are excellent when it comes to reducing anxiety by making them calmer and more focused on what happens inside them.

Teach them to Foster Gratitude

Now that the children are older, they can appreciate what gratitude brings to the mental health table. The Montessori philosophy advises practicing several forms of gratitude.

These can be anything from keeping a gratitude journal to enrolling in a gratitude circle. Indeed, it is a true eye-opener, as they can see all the positive aspects of their lives. Moreover, when they are filled with this amazing grateful feeling and appreciate what they have, they will be able to reduce any negative depressive and anxious emotions seamlessly.

Create a Supportive Environment

You already know how imperative it is to have a safe and supporting environment for your child, and this should be your priority through every development age. Naturally, when your child feels heard and supported, they will express their feelings openly. When it comes to dealing with anxiety and depression, the battle will be half-won.

Get them to spend some Time in Nature

Nothing heals like nature. Allowing older children to engage with the natural world will work wonders for their mental health. The Montessori method encourages making camping trips, doing some outdoor learning activities, or even a simple nature walk will be beneficial. Learning and becoming more aware of nature's wisdom and peace will undoubtedly assist them in managing anxiety.

Finally, it is time for some Self-Care

Older children can now understand more about taking care of themselves and nurturing their overall well-being. Therefore, it is vital to practice this with them. For instance, explain how getting enough sleep or eating well can benefit their health. Furthermore, encourage them to indulge in activities that truly make them feel joyful and fulfilled. By practicing this, they will prioritize their mental health and help them manage any depressive or anxious thoughts.

Chapter 17: Community and Socialization in a Montessori Environment

The Montessori philosophy doesn't only focus on the child as a sole individual. Although it's very concerned with its development to become independent individuals, it also points out the importance of socialization and community. Every person feels the need to belong to a certain group. Although some have a greater urge for this than others, I bet you can't think of anyone who wants to rely completely on their own.

The Montessori method encourages students to explore their own needs and interests but also to share them with their peers, family, or other people in their environment. It often claims that, for the child to learn as much as possible, they need to participate in different communities where they'll be able to express their views but also hear the opinions of others. This is the only way they can further develop their critical thinking and the ability to stand up for themselves when their opinions are challenged.

Explanation of the Importance of Community and Socialization in Montessori Education

How important are the notions of community and socialization really? You've often heard that you should encourage your children to socialize and actively participate in a community, but you might wonder how important this act really is. For that reason, I'm here to give you an in-depth insight into the topic so you'll learn why your child needs to experience both.

The Importance of Community in Montessori

The founder of the Montessori approach, Dr. Maria Montessori, saw the connection between student's emotional development and their ability to learn effectively. To properly support this relationship, she developed the concept of a community that's supposed to support their social skills and academic achievement. Looking back, the community has been crucial to the Montessori approach since the very beginning. Although this notion might mean different things (your prepared home/family environment or a school classroom), the main goal of each is to be a place where the child will feel comfortable and in control. This means that, inside their community, they'll be provided with all the resources they need to grow and develop following the Montessori principles. In addition, they should also show responsibility and contribute to this environment by working on their skills and succeeding in various challenges.

Children should see the community they're part of as a place of growth and support. It should be an environment where they'll be properly challenged and given access to different resources they'll use for their advancement. In this community, they should feel free to explore their interests, experiment with different ideas, and do creative tasks not only by themselves but with their peers. One of the main traits that this environment should teach them is to be respectful and patient and to see other kids as their equals. Your child needs to see that everyone's effort matters and to embrace and support the work of others.

Group and teamwork are a couple of things that are also deeply encouraged in the Montessori community. This is because it's been proven that children can experience numerous benefits from this type of work, as they often step forward to offer guidance to others as they work together to find a solution. Sometimes, they can also be put in groups while working on more challenging material. This helps them understand the material better and strengthens the bond between them. This creates a feeling of incorporated family values, which greatly impact their development.

So, you've been able to see the positive impact that comes out of children feeling like they belong to a community. Now, let's discover the importance of socialization in the Montessori environment and see the range of impact it has on the child's development.

The Importance of Socialization in Montessori

The Montessori philosophy focuses on the child's education and various other skills they'll find useful throughout their lives. This is the main thing that separates this approach from the traditional one, as the child is taught to focus on every aspect—cognitive, emotional, and ultimately, social.

We are all social creatures by nature. It's in our character that we're always searching for communication and connection and a way to establish different types of relationships with the people around us. Just like grown-ups, children experience the same need for socialization, which is why it's such an important aspect of Montessori philosophy.

The Montessori approach is focused on encouraging students to learn and socialize with their peers, which is primarily done by introducing freedom within limits. It's been proven that children learn best when they're put in a social environment, meaning that they're not forbidden interaction and liberty of choice, so they can explore many activities. They're also led toward being respectful and kind when socializing.

Being in a social environment allows children to express their ideas in front of others and hear what the rest have to say. With the help of others, they can learn more about themselves by discussing various opinions and using critical thinking. This type of setting is ideal for boosting children's development as it provides many socialization opportunities, which is the key to shaping children into communicative and respectful individuals.

When it comes to the prepared Montessori environment, you need to know that social development comes in many forms, some of which include:

Mixed age groups

Dr. Montessori strongly believed in the importance of socialization and the power of learning from one another. For this reason, she made mixed-age groups the basis of her approach because it further fosters this need for communication and guidance. In this type of environment, it's not unusual to notice that an older child is helping a younger one understand and finish a certain activity. This is one of the best ways they can gain social maturity because they're directly put in the role of a guide.

This type of social environment allows children to learn from one another and removes the pressure to compete. Instead, they feel more motivated to collaborate and socialize, being mindful of their interactions.

Small group lessons

Even though the Montessori principles are focused on each child's individual growth, some lessons can still be presented to small groups. This type of setting is great for initiating discussions and helping children socialize that way. Moreover, it creates a safe environment that makes students feel comfortable when expressing their thoughts and ideas among their peers. Aside from making children more sociable, it helps them improve their conversational skills and understanding.

Lessons in good behavior

A very important component of every socialization process is that children learn how to show courtesy and fineness. The basis of every positive relationship is mutual respect, and students need to know how to act appropriately when engaging in dialogue—especially if they're presenting opposing ideas.

This is the beauty of the Montessori approach—since it teaches children what respect means, they become more capable of resolving issues and promoting peace and collaboration.

Discussion of How to Create a Community and Socialization Opportunities in a Home Environment

As a parent, you want your child to grow in an environment that offers optimal healthy development opportunities. This does not only apply to their school setting but also their home environment. Knowing the importance of community and socialization for every child, it's only natural that you'll want to practice them at home. But how do you create such opportunities when your family setting is much smaller compared to their school?

Fortunately, there are several aspects you can focus on that will promote these processes. Of course, you'll need to adapt your home environment to meet the Montessori principles in a way that respects your child's needs and social skills. Here are a few ideas on how you can create socialization and community opportunities for your child at home:

Promote independence

It's at the core of the Montessori approach to promoting independence in children, teaching them to be self-reliant and critical as they're growing up. For that reason, one of the first things you should do is encourage them to be responsible for their tasks. Out in the community, this could be simple tasks like picking trash up off the ground when you see it, helping someone who dropped something, or inviting other kids to play at the park. This will not only help them grow into independent people but will also encourage their social skills.

Encourage their involvement in a community

Motivate your child to participate in the community by engaging in different activities. They can achieve this by volunteering or taking part in community events. Doing this from a young age will help them work on their sense of social responsibility and will further encourage community involvement.

Create a mix-aged community

As I've already mentioned, children learn best when they're a part of mixed-age communities. For that reason, you should try to create such one in your own home. This is quite easy because it involves communicating with their older or younger siblings, friends, and neighbors. It will give them the opportunity to work on their social skills, as well as to guide or learn from others.

Inspire social play

The Montessori philosophy is very determined about the importance of social play as children grow. For that reason, you should motivate your kids to play with their siblings and friends, as this is crucial for the development of many positive traits they'll use throughout their lives. Focus on involving them in games that promote cooperation and inspire them to train their teamwork and social abilities.

Promote peer-learning

Similarly to what I've mentioned above, children often acquire knowledge better when they learn from their peers. To promote this valuable activity, encourage them to share their experience and knowledge with others and learn from them.

Include them in real-life experiences

Another very important thing the Montessori teaching focuses on is the development of real-life skills that children will use long after they finish their formal education, i.e., when they become adults. So, it's very important that you provide different opportunities for your child to learn these skills from a young age. Consider involving them in the realization of various daily household activities. Depending on their age and abilities, these can include meal prep, cooking, gardening, cleaning, etc.

Encourage group work

Group Work and teamwork are two very important aspects of the Montessori environment. Although this approach focuses on children's individual growth, it encourages them to participate in group activities to promote the development of different skills. In your home, you can dedicate a space where your child can engage in group play, such as reading or playing games. This will encourage both social interaction and collaboration skills.

Include them in social events

As social beings, teaching your children the importance of participating in social events from a very young age is crucial.

In your home, you can think about organizing a game night or dinner where your family will gather to spend quality time together. You can even invite your friends or family members who don't live with you to participate in these social gatherings. They're all great ways to develop your child's social and communication skills.

Promote good communication and conflict-resolution skills

Effective communication is key to resolving all kinds of conflicts, which is why the Montessori philosophy greatly emphasizes those. You should teach your child, from the youngest of age, to be clear when expressing their feelings and opinions, but to do it respectfully. Give them opportunities to practice conflict-resolution skills so they'll be prepared for the future.

Suggestions for Finding and Participating in Montessori-Inspired Community Events and Activities

I've already mentioned in a few paragraphs above that you should encourage your children to participate in community events and activities. But they're not the only ones to experience various benefits from participating in such. As a parent, you should research and find different Montessori-inspired groups and events you'll benefit from participating in. These will all provide unique opportunities for you to get in touch with other parents using this approach to raising their children, so you'll get to exchange tips and experiences that will help you improve your approach.

Have a look at the following suggestions for Montessori-inspired events you should consider being a part of:

Local Montessori schools

One of the first things you should consider is whether there's a Montessori school where you live or nearby. These schools often organize community events and activities open to the public. This is probably the easiest way to take part in a Montessori-inspired event, so make sure that you check their website or social media page for any upcoming events.

Montessori parent groups

You might be surprised how many parents already raise their children following the Montessori approach. You can check whether there are any parent groups in your town by searching for local groups on social media or through different community organizations. If you find any, feel free to connect with them and attend the events or meetings they organize. I'm sure they'll be eager to share their own and learn from your personal experience so that you can consider if there's room for improvement in your parenting method.

Workshops and conferences

These also offer great opportunities for you to broaden your knowledge about the Montessori philosophy and connect with other families interested in or practicing this approach. Check if there's a local Montessori organization near you, or perhaps a national one, and attend their hosting events.

Montessori educators

Another way to get in touch with other parents tailoring their parenting method according to the Montessori principles is to ask a Montessori educator whether they know some. The odds are that someone has already reached out to them with the same request, so they might be able to get in touch with them. Moreover, you can ask these educators whether they're familiar with any community events or activities that are happening in your area that you can attend.

Host your own event

Lastly, regardless of whether there are any community activities in your area, you can decide to host your own and gather with other parents who are going through the same process as you. You can organize playdates for your children or meetups and outdoor events for the grown-ups and talk about different topics that interest you. Speak from your experience and listen to what others have to share to see whether there's something you're willing to implement into your own parenting method. Plus, this will allow you to meet many new people and broaden your social circle.

Chapter 18:
Special Situations

The Montessori philosophy has proven incredibly beneficial for children of all ages. Its unique approach to creating the optimal thriving environment that supports children's development is the main reason why so many parents are trying to incorporate it into their parenting techniques. If you've carefully read this book so far, you've learned that Montessori principles apply to kids of all ages. They work on supporting their optimal developmental process, fostering responsibility and independence. But can these principles be used on children with special needs?

I decided to dedicate this whole chapter to answering this question so you'll see how beneficial Montessori is for these kids.

Children With Special Needs

First things first, allow me to answer the question briefly. Yes, the Montessori approach can be applied when teaching and parenting children with special needs. This approach allows them to feel safe and comfortable in the prepared environment primarily focused on nurturing and understanding them. Due to the nature of the Montessori philosophy, the approach is meant to be tailored to the needs and abilities of every child, allowing them to grow and learn at their own pace. Looking at it from this aspect, it's easy to conclude that it can be way more beneficial than any traditional approach.

Understanding the Montessori Approach to Special Needs

As you already know, every child is different in every aspect, from the pace at which they develop to the way and speed they learn new information. This is the main reason so many parents are interested in implementing its principles in their parenting method, as it allows for full adaptability toward their child's requirements. And this directly reflects the main goal of the Montessori mission—to allow full freedom to explore and develop without feeling the pressure of falling behind. Instead, they will feel confident in their way of progressing without needing to compare with others.

Another advantage of using the Montessori approach in raising children with special needs is that it won't leave space for them to be discriminated against by other students. Instead of being indicated as students who have a harder time acquiring the learning material, they'll be given the opportunity to advance at their own pace. This is very easy to achieve because, through this approach, all of their needs and requirements are considered. For example, if they're using another technique to acquire their subjects' material compared to the rest of their peers, they won't be forced to use the others' method. Instead, they'll be given freedom and resources to support their own way of learning, all with the goal of helping them develop at the pace they feel most comfortable with.

As you can tell, the Montessori approach aims at providing each child with optimal thriving conditions so they'll reach their maximum capacity at a given time. As a parent who wants to incorporate this philosophy in supporting their child's development, you need to think about how to adapt your parenting approach to provide optimal support.

Another thing you need to know about Montessori philosophy is that it doesn't only focus on the child's academic development. Instead, it cares to include everything that plays an important role in their growth, including their social and psychological development. Based on numerous research, children should be carefully observed and taught practical life skills they'll use throughout their lives. This also includes guiding them in forming relationships and establishing meaningful communication with their peers so they can easily develop a sense of belonging in the environment. (Sunny Day Talbert, 2020)

Although this philosophy wasn't specifically developed to support children with special needs, it also wasn't made for those without disabilities, either. Following are a few examples of how Montessori can help in supporting children with different disabilities:

Autism

Autism is a very specific type of developmental disability that doesn't look the same in different children. While some don't experience any major challenges, others find it quite hard to deal with the simplest everyday tasks. Montessori is beneficial for them because its personalized approach allows for adjusting the living and learning environment to the kids' unique needs. Research shows that it's all about creating a setting tailored to their abilities and promoting learning and growth at their own pace. (Ya-Chih Chang, Jill Locke, 2016)

ADHD

ADHD is another developmental disorder that can negatively affect the child's development if placed in an unfavorable environment. These kids are too easily distracted by their surroundings because their ability to focus on their tasks is significantly lowered. According to studies, Montessori is great for supporting their development because it allows adults to design the environment in a way that eliminates all major distractions, allowing students to easily focus on their learning experience. (Eugenia G. Gkeka, 2018)

Speech delay

The adaptable nature of this philosophy makes it suitable for children with speech delays, as well. So, the environment in which your child learns and grows can be tailored to its unique speech needs and offer enough support to work on improving them. At the same time, it won't cause any frustration or discomfort to the child because they'll be given suitable opportunities to develop.

Sensory processing disorder

Children with sensory processing disorder can have a really hard time adapting to the traditional schooling environment. Instead, they may feel left out or willingly retract from any involvement or even develop a negative behavior toward the setting. Implementing the Montessori principles gives children a more advantageous thriving environment where all major stimulants will be removed or controlled. This means that the child will learn to be aware of and control their senses, reducing the possibility of a negative experience.

Dyslexia

Dyslexia, being a language-based condition, is mostly related to the child's ability to read and write. For that reason, children will benefit from being placed in an environment that reduces the pressure to develop their language abilities faster and will provide the optimal environment for advancing at their own pace.

Homeschooling

Many parents have or are still considering the idea of homeschooling, considering whether that will provide their children with a more beneficial learning environment. As a parent of a child with special needs, I understand that your concern has increased. This isn't only because you're worried your child will be bullied by other children or pushed away from the classroom community. It's also because you're afraid that they won't adapt to the pace of acquiring new material and will feel left out.

And for many parents, this can turn out to be true to an extent. But if you're already interested in trying out the Montessori approach and creating a home environment that's completely catered to your child's needs, then I have good news for you. This is. Indeed, something you can achieve, but before you start planning for it, you need to know several important things.

Montessori Homeschooling

If you already have some knowledge and practice with homeschooling, the odds are that you've already implemented the majority of the methods that Montessori philosophy suggests. The most important thing you need to know about Montessori homeschooling is that the child and their own needs direct it. This doesn't mean that you should completely abandon the use of a curriculum and learning materials, but you should implement it in a way that gives optimal support to your child's development. Furthermore, studies show that you should spend some time creating a prepared environment that will encourage your child to freely explore and discover around the limits you've initially set. (Maria Eva Chaffin, 2019)

Don't expect to come across a curriculum you can follow from start to end. Even though some are designed specifically with the Montessori approach in mind, they should serve more as guidance points than something you need to follow step by step. This is because Montessori is more of a philosophy than a set of rules you should follow, giving you more freedom to create a curriculum that aligns with your child's requirements. Remember, each child is characterized by their individual needs and interests, so your homeschooling approach should revolve around those. One of the best things to create a home Montessori curriculum is to gather plenty of materials, have them in hand, and later decide which ones will make the best choice.

Speaking of gathering various Montessori materials, know that this doesn't mean you should buy every book and every interactive game out there that can be suitable for your homeschooling setting. There are, in fact, many materials that you can prepare on your own, which will help you save on resources. The best part? These types of materials can tend to several areas you need to exercise, including language, sensorial, math, cultural, etc.

Here are a few things you need to keep in mind when designing the Montessori homeschooling environment for your child:

No lesson planning

One of the first things you need to know before you consider implementing this teaching method is that you can forget about lesson planning. Instead of coming up with strict lesson plans to follow, your attention will be more focused on observing how your child progresses day to day. Of course, you can think of several concepts and ideas your child should work on refining, but you can't possibly predict how fast they will achieve that. All you have to do is think of a method to help them acquire the material more easily.

Spending time outdoors

Research supports the fact that another very important aspect of any Montessori homeschooling is the value of spending time in an outdoor environment. This doesn't only mean that you should encourage them to spend time in nature but also to interact with other children. You might be amazed by how much they can learn by interacting with other kids. (Nimal Vaz)

Learning takes place all the time

Instead of deciding that learning will take place in a strict time frame, Montessori homeschooling states that learning should happen all the time. Just because it allows more freedom to tailor the curriculum according to your child's specific needs, it means that it can take place anywhere at any time. The Montessori philosophy looks at learning as something that happens at every moment of every day, not a fixed-period activity.

Montessori homeschooling is incredibly different from a traditional classroom

Although I'm quite sure that you already know this, I need to point out that the Montessori homeschooling environment is entirely different from the traditional classroom you're used to. We begin by presenting information to them as parents, not as teachers, which completely shifts their perspective of this situation.

Homeschooling can be more affordable

Montessori homeschooling largely depends on the materials you're going to present to your children. And as I've already mentioned, this doesn't mean you have to buy every book or game you come across. There are many options for you to create interactive materials on your own, which is what you should do instead. In the long term, this will not only save you money but will also directly include you in the process of designing activities for them.

Transitioning to a Traditional School

So, preparing a home Montessori environment so your child can attend homeschooling can't last forever. They will eventually have to switch to a traditional school where they'll be able to further broaden their knowledge on topics you can't really explain at home. And the same thing applies to kids who have potentially attended a Montessori school setting outside of your home.

And as every parent, you must be worried about this change and how it will affect your child. After spending so much time in one environment, it can be challenging to transition into another. But with the right support and preparation, this shouldn't be a dreadful thing at all. Studies show that you, as a parent, can do several things to support this change in your child's life and make it easier. (Elizabeth Lapon, 2020)

Supporting Change

Children who have grown up in a Montessori environment are used to doing things differently than those who haven't.

This can confuse them once they leave their current environment and enter a traditional classroom. This transition from having complete freedom to move and explore to having to remain seated most of the time and asking for permission before doing anything can be confusing for many. As a parent, it's your responsibility to prepare your child for this change by explaining what they should expect. After all, they've been raised to be considerate of their environment and to show respect, so they shouldn't protest about having to listen to their new teachers.

The good news is that most children who underwent this transition between a Montessori and a traditional environment didn't find it too hard to adapt. While they might've felt bored at first or have trouble understanding why each child has to do the same thing at the same time, the odds are that it won't be long before they adapt to the new setting. Most of them go through this process fairly quickly, as soon as they make new friends and begin communicating and playing with them.

But this transition from a Montessori to a traditional schooling environment doesn't only concern a single aspect of the child's development. Despite the educational one, these children also significantly change their social life. Not only have Montessori students received greater freedom in choosing their learning materials and exercises, but they also didn't take any standardized tests. This might be one of the greatest differences between these two approaches, but luckily, it's proven that children adapt quickly to the new way of testing their knowledge.

When it comes to social transitioning, Montessori children are able to notice quite some differences between their previous and new environments. So far, they have been taught about different traits they'll find useful throughout their life, such as respect, courtesy, solving conflicts, making decisions, and so much more. And it is these skills that will prove to be very beneficial when making this important school change.

As a parent, there are several things you can do to support your child and make a more effortless shift:

Plan the transition

The first thing you should do is start planning your child's transition from a Montessori to a traditional classroom environment. This is the best way to reduce the stress they're expected to experience and give them a heads-up about the changes that will come. Let them ask questions and try to answer as many as possible so they'll be informed about what they can expect from their new environment. However, make sure you're helping them form realistic expectations so they don't end up disappointed or demotivated after some time.

Help your child see the advantages of being in a new environment

Every change in life comes with some positive aspects, this one included. And your child must understand those so they'll embrace the change. You can tell them about how meeting new children and forming new friendships can be positive, as well as how the new environment will help them broaden their current knowledge and introduce them to new ideas.

Talk to the teachers

Another thing you should do as a parent is talk to the teacher that will work with your child. Explain the situation so they will understand what they can expect to deal with. This might even help them come up with their own plan that will help speed up your child's transition.

Discuss different assignments

Doing homework and studying for tests are probably the two things that your child will be able to notice from the very beginning. And since this is probably something they've never done, it can be hard to determine how they'll adapt. Speak to them and even offer your assistance at the beginning so they'll see that this isn't something very hard to do.

Support their independence at home

Although your child is now actively participating in their traditional learning environment, it doesn't mean that you can't continue practicing the Montessori principles at home. There are many ways you can support their development following this approach when they're spending their time at home, so why don't you do your own research and see how you can support them this way?

Don't compare!

Lastly, don't forget that it's never a good idea to compare your children with others, regardless of whether you're using the other students as a positive or a negative example. Each child is unique, and you should always embrace that. If they need a boost, try to think of other ways to motivate them instead of comparing them to others, as the latter can only cause negative feelings and unwanted behavior.

Multilingual Homes

It's not uncommon for a child to grow up in a multilingual home, especially if they have parents or grandparents from another area, speaking a different language from the one native to a country. This unique situation has many benefits, as children are exposed to different cultural influences, which will help them gain a deeper understanding of the world's diversity. Moreover, bi or multilingual children have improved cognitive function and enjoy a greater ability to focus on learning. Moreover, they're often praised for their great memory skills and enhanced problem-solving abilities.

Given these many advantages, you're probably wondering when's the best time to expose your child to a second language. As Dr. Montessori had observed, the 'sensitive period' in which the child has the greatest capacity to acquire language is between birth right until they turn 6. This means that it's never too early to actively engage your child in a bilingual or multilingual environment. Even if your child is older than this, it's still possible for them to experience the benefits of knowing more than one language. Although it will probably take a little more time for them to learn the new language, nothing is impossible if they're dedicated to achieving this goal.

Methods of raising a multilingual child

Now, if you're interested in raising your child in a multilingual environment, it's important that you're aware of the methods that will help them get the most out of it. You can't just place it there and hope they'll acquire the new language on their own. Based on research (Romali Rosales Chavarría, 2021), here's what you can do instead:

- **One person, one language**

As you can tell by the name, this approach states that each person in the family will speak in their own language. This is a great method to use in a home setting where both parents speak different languages, allowing the child to learn both languages simultaneously.

- **Minority language**

If you decide to use this approach, then it means that all family members should use the minority language at home. You're allowed to speak the community language when you're outside of your house. This is applicable only if both parents can speak the minority language fluently, and the child will be able to learn the community language at school and when playing with their friends.

- **The context method**

Also known as the method of "time and place," this method requires that you speak two or more languages at different times. Also, you can use different languages to speak in a specific situation; for example, speaking one in the morning and one in the evening or switching the language depending on the room in your house you're in.

- **Mixed language environment**

When it comes to this method, there are no set rules that you can use. Instead, you'll use two or more languages interchangeably and not depending on a different situation. Both you and your partner should feel free to change between different languages when you see fit.

But even if your child is growing up in a monolingual environment, it doesn't mean that there aren't ways for you to introduce a second language. If none of you are fluent in another language, you can expose your child to a foreign one by enrolling them in a language class or encouraging them to watch movies or listen to music. Moreover, if you have a friend or family member who speaks another language, you can get your child to spend time with them.

The method you'll ultimately choose to use will entirely depend on your specific situation. So, consider all your options and choose the one you feel will be most convenient. Try to be as consistent as possible with the method you're practicing, but don't hesitate to change the approach if you feel it's not working for you and your child. Moreover, you can also consider starting to learn a foreign language (if you don't already know one). This will allow you to directly support your child as they acquire new language skills, and you can even practice it together.

Conclusions

We've come to the end of this book. Thank you for taking the time to read my insights and work on becoming a better parent. Together, we can shape a brighter future for our loved ones!

If you carefully read everything you thought would benefit you, you now know the goal of "The Complete Guide to Raising a Montessori Child." It is specially curated to serve as a comprehensive resource for any parent who wants to employ the Montessori method, regardless of whether they want this for their child's schooling or to implement it in their parenting approach at home. However, I also wanted to start with the basics of the Montessori method and dive deeper into its philosophy to help you build the right mindset. In addition, I felt obliged to explain more about your role as a parent and the roles of other adults in your child's surroundings, plus how you can affect self-paced learning in a safe and supportive environment.

Furthermore, I've addressed every stage of development separately to clearly guide you no matter your child's age period. By encapsulating all the practical strategies and tips in my book, my purpose was for you to find a parenting companion who is always there to suggest all the best practices for your child. From toddlers to young adults, the book is filled with ideas to help children become self-directed and independent learners, always ready with skills that will bring them only success. Prepare to completely transform your parenting by implementing these Montessori principles in your day-to-day activities.

At its very core, this guide will thoroughly prepare your child for the future by establishing a Montessori-created environment and promoting various skills like communication, independence, and problem-solving. But what sets my book apart is the complete attention to every stage, including the teen and young adult period—which are incredibly challenging for many parents. After all, when raising your infant, toddler, preschooler, or tween, they will all enter different stages, so you have to be prepared to tackle those ages seamlessly. Therefore, among many other things, I wrote about how to help them foster independence, support self-reflection, and promote collaboration at home.

I also discussed technology and how it can be used for good, followed by an in-depth analysis of how important community and socialization are for the Montessori environment. It was vital to tap into special situations and explain how this philosophy can entirely benefit your child. Most importantly, I addressed mental health challenges such as anxiety and depression in children and offered solutions for younger and older ones.

To conclude, this book is completely tailored to Montessori philosophy. It's not just a guide to provide a short-term solution but a roadmap to ensure your child grows in a supportive and nurturing environment. My parting thoughts are that with this Montessori method and everything I have talked about so far, you will be able to help your child reach its full potential. Which parent doesn't want to see their child evolve into a perfectly happy, fulfilled, and healthy individual? Now you can, too, and the best part? You don't even have to send them to a Montessori school to do that—you have everything you need here.

Appendix:
Lists of Useful Websites and Other Resources

1. Montessori Philosophy and History

   - https://amshq.org/About-Montessori/History-of-Montessori/Who-Was-Maria-Montessori
   - https://www.international-montessori.org/en/child-centered-schools-belgium-the-montessori-approach/

2. Montessori Method

   - https://montessoriacademy.com.au/montessori-education/montessori-learning-materials/#:~:text=Montessori%20materials%20are%20hands%2Don,independent%20learning%20and%20problem%2Dsolving

- https://themontessorinotebook.com/montessori-approach-to-discipline
- https://montessorimessage.net/tag/self-awareness/

3. Montessori Home Environment

- https://www.fishtownmontessori.com/how-to-create-a-montessori-friendly-home/
- https://www.berkshiremontessori.org/msb-blog/7ways-montessori-home-environment
- https://sapientiamontessori.com/montessori/montessori-at-home/

4. Montessori Infants

- https://www.guidepostmontessori.com/blog/montessori-for-babies-complete-beginners-guide
- https://www.guidepostmontessori.com/blog/discipline-tips-montessori-perspective
- https://momtessorilife.com/2017/06/15/20-montessori-inspired-sensorial-activities-for-infants-and-toddlers/

- https://masterthemontessorilife.com/8-easy-montessori-culture-activities

- https://www.montessoridaoshi.com/single-post/2019/11/05/math-and-the-infanttoddler

- https://www.stcathmont.org/apps/pages/index.jsp?uREC_ID=1424528&type=d&pREC_ID=1592083#:~:text=When%20the%20child%20first%20enters,the%20capabilities%20of%20that%20child

5. Montessori Toddlers

- https://www.dailymontessori.com/montessori-age-12-24-months/

- https://aimmontessoriteachertraining.org/montessori-stages-of-development-for-early-learning/

- https://genevamontessori.org/should-be-able-to-do-at-2-years-old/

- https://www.redrosemontessori.com/program/montessori-programs/

- https://momtessorilife.com/2017/04/14/10-montessori-inspired-math-activities-for-toddlers/

- https://piklertrianglediy.com/montessori-cultural-activities/
- https://thetoddlerplaybook.com/montessori-language-literacy-activities/
- https://www.montessorinature.com/help-young-children-regulate-emotions/
- https://www.melanatedmontessori.com/post/setting-boundaries-and-limits-the-montessori-way
- https://reachformontessori.com/10-tips-to-stop-toddler-tantrums/

6. Montessori Preschoolers & School-Age

- https://montessorifortoday.com/what-are-montessori-activities-examples-for-every-age/
- https://puffinsschoolofmontessori.wordpress.com/2015/11/11/3-to-4-year-olds-developmental-milestones/
- https://calgarypreschools.ca/blog/Why+Do+We+Focus+On+Play+In+A+Montessori+Preschool+Program/139

- https://www.whatdowedoallday.com/practical-life-activities-for-kids/
- https://www.thinkamajigs.com/blog/4-popular-montessori-sensorial-activities-for-preschoolers/
- https://www.oakgrovelearning.com/sensorial-life-activities-for-preschoolers/
- https://mybrightonmontessori.com/setting-limits-using-the-montessori-approach/
- https://silverlinemontessori.com/four-planes-of-development-in-a-montessori-school/
- https://www.thoughtco.com/montessori-method-4774801#:~:text=Montessori's%20theory%20identifies%20four%20planes,18%2D24%20years%20old
- https://colegiomillaray.com/en/10-keys-montessori-limits/
- https://www.fishtownmontessori.com/a-look-at-discipline-the-montessori-way/
- https://mumslittleexplorers.com/montessori-practical-lifea-activities-kids/
- https://carrotsareorange.com/montessori-math-activities-lessons/

- https://www.fishtownmontessori.com/montessori-language-activities-for-home/

7. Montessori Tweens

- https://www.mildenhallmontessori.com/lower-elementary
- https://aimmontessoriteachertraining.org/mind-six-twelve-year-old/
- https://www.berkshiremontessori.org/msb-blog/montessori-for-adolescents
- https://hershey-montessori.org/what-do-adolescents-need-right-now/
- http://www.lamplighterschool.org/social-emotional-development
- https://multisori.com/blogs/getting-started-with-montessori/a-montessori-approach-to-discipline
- https://www.howwemontessori.com/how-we-montessori/2018/03/montessori-at-home-activities-for-my-10-year-old.html

- https://maitlandmontessori.org/our-school/9-12-years-old

8. Montessori Teens

- https://themontessorifamily.com/montessori-parenting-are-your-ready-for-the-teenage-years/
- https://www.williamsburgmontessori.org/blog/empowering-adolescents-the-advantages-of-montessori-education-for-teenagers/
- https://blog.hudsonmontessori.org/montessori-parenting-a-teenager/

9. Montessori College Age & Young Adults

- https://blog.fms.org/does-a-montessori-education-prepare-students-for-college
- https://medium.com/taking-note/how-the-montessori-method-applies-to-todays-workplace-419c37f719fa#:~:text=The%20Montessori%20Method%20trusts%20that,It%20works%20for%20adults%2C%20too.

10. Montessori Technology Use

- https://forestbluffschool.org/screen-time-and-your-childs-development-a-montessori-perspective/
- https://themontessorifamily.com/montessori-parenting-13-tips-to-reduce-and-manage-screen-time/

11. Montessori Community and Socialization

- https://montessoriacademysharonsprings.com/social-development-in-a-montessori-school/
- https://montessoriacademy.com.au/montessori-and-classroom-communities/

12. Montessori Special Situations

- https://montessorifortoday.com/is-montessori-good-for-children-with-special-needs/
- https://www.time4learning.com/homeschooling-styles/montessori.html#:~:text=With%20a%20Mo

ntessori%20homeschool%2C%20the,students%20t
o%20explore%20and%20discover

- https://www.childoftheredwoods.com/articles/secr
ets-montessori-homeschooling

13. Montessori and Transitioning to a Traditional School

- https://montessorischoolofwestminster.org/what-happens-when-students-move-on-to-other-schools-after-being-in-a-montessori-classroom/
- https://montessori-academy.com/blog/transition-into-montessori-schooling/
- https://aimmontessoriteachertraining.org/faq-how-will-my-child-adjust-to-traditional-school-after-being-in-montessori-school/
- https://www.wacomontessorischool.org/transition-montessori-traditional-schools-will-child-adjust/

14. Montessori Multilingual Children

- https://montessoriacademy.com.au/raising-multilingual-children/

15. Montessori Mental Health Challenges

- https://theglobalmontessorinetwork.org/what-does-research-indicate-about-academic-achievement-and-emotional-wellbeing-of-montessori-students/
- https://www.mariamontessori.org/montessori-educated-children-are-happier-adults/
- https://therapytips.org/articles/montessori-education-promotes-psychological-well-being
- https://applemontessorischools.com/blog/strategies-to-recognize-and-cope-with-your-childs-anxiety
- https://www.researchgate.net/publication/298205328_Integrating_Montessori_Principles_In_Mental_Health_Education
- https://amshq.org/Blog/2022-10-14-Ways-to-Support-Infant-and-Toddler-Mental-Health

Author's Information

Beatrice Bell is a mother and retired Montessori kindergarten teacher who now spends her days writing books on parenting advice. She lives in Florida with her two cats and partner. She loves reading mysteries on her hammock and working in her garden. She is also an avid traveler and loves organizing family vacations, especially to countries where she can practice her Spanish.

Printed in Dunstable, United Kingdom

67558256R00188